GUITAR TAB EDITION

ROCK GUITAR

SONGBOOK · VOLUME 1   1950s–1970s

T0055413

Produced by
Alfred Music Publishing Co., Inc.
P.O. Box 10003
Van Nuys, CA 91410-0003
alfred.com

Printed in USA.

ISBN-10: 0-7390-8593-X
ISBN-13: 978-0-7390-8593-6

Cover guitar photo courtesy of Gibson USA
Star pattern background art courtesy of webtreats.mysitemyway.com

 Alfred Cares. Contents printed on 100% recycled paper.

ARTIST INDEX

CONTENTS

25 OR 6 TO 4

Moderately fast ♩ = 146

Words and Music by
ROBERT LAMM

25 or 6 to 4 - 11 - 1

search - ing   for_____   some   things_____   to   say._____
get - ting   up_____   to   splash_____   my   face._____
spin - ning   room_____   is   sink - ing_____   deep._____

Horns

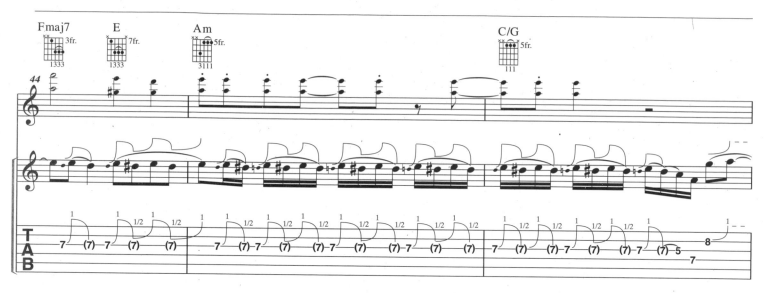

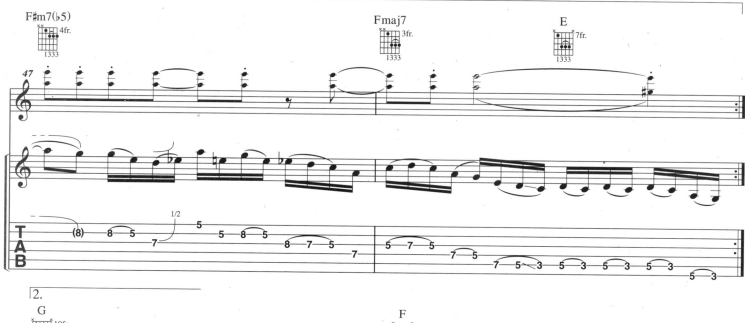

Guitar Solo:

⊕ *Coda*

Outro:
w/Rhy. Fig. 1 *(Elec. Gtrs. 1 & 2)*

twen-ty - five___ or six___ to four.___

Elec. Gtr. 3

*Dm(9)   Cm(9)

Elec. Gtr. 3 tacet
Horns

Elec. Gtrs. 1 & 2

*Chords are implied.

B6(♯9)   G7/B♭   B/A

molto rit.

AMIE

Words and Music by
CRAIG LEE FULLER

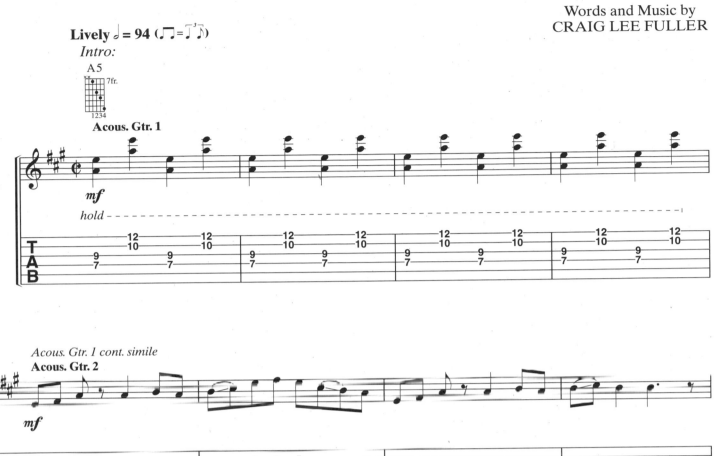

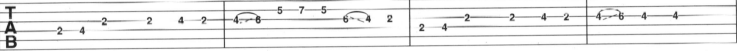

Amie - 11 - 1

But   now   you're   off   with   some - one___   else,___   and   I'm___   a - lone.___
which   way   we should   turn,   to - geth - er,   or___   a - lone?___
that   I   don't know   if___   it's___   you   or if___   it's   me.___

___   You see, I   thought   that I___   might___   keep   you for___   my___
___   I can   nev - er   see___   what's___   right   or   what   is___
___   If it's   one   of us___   I'm___   sure   we both___   will___

20

Chorus:

24

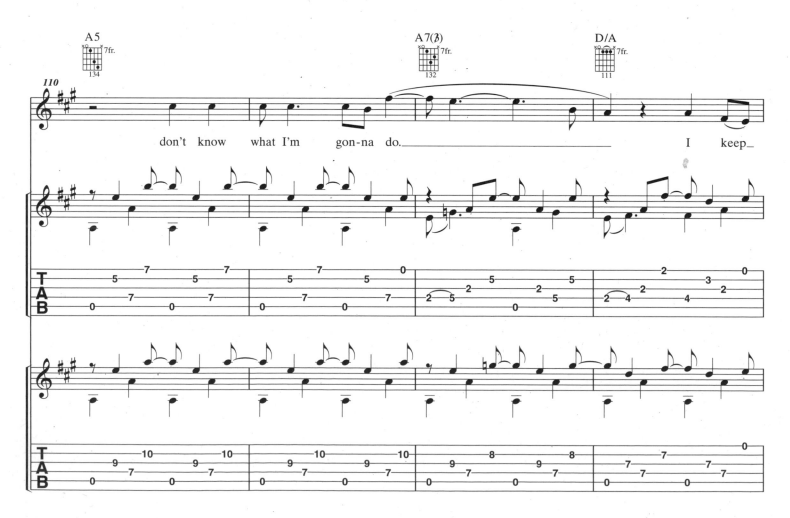

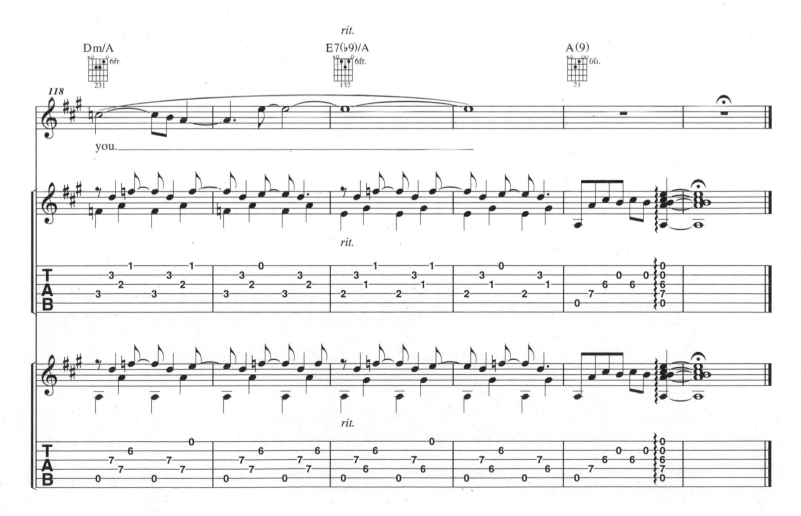

BLACK WATER

Words and Music by
PATRICK SIMMONS

2. Well, if it

Guitar Solo:

w/Rhy. Fig. 1 *(Acous. Gtr. 1) cont. simile, 5 times*

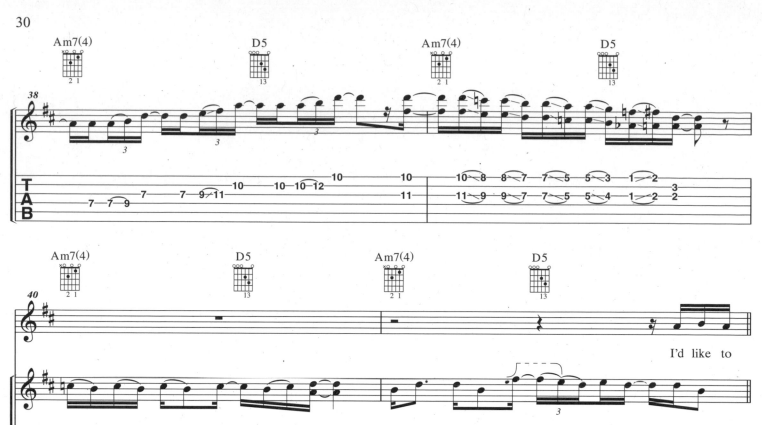

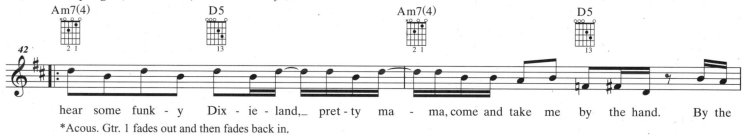

Outro:

w/Rhy. Fig. 1 *(Acous. Gtr. 1) cont. simile till fade*

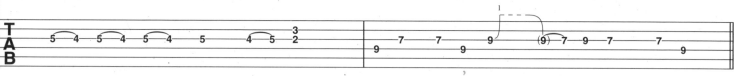

hear some funk-y Dix-ie-land,_ pret-ty ma-ma, come and take me by the hand. By the
*Acous. Gtr. 1 fades out and then fades back in.

Repeat ad lib. and fade

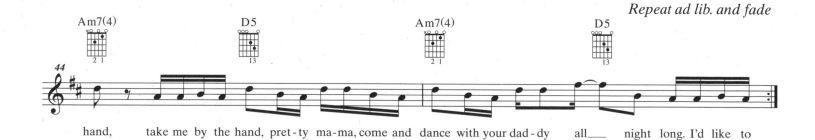

hand, take me by the hand, pret-ty ma-ma, come and dance with your dad-dy all__ night long. I'd like to

Verse 2:
Well, if it rains, I don't care,
Don't make no difference to me;
Just take that streetcar that's goin' uptown.
Yeah, I'd like to hear some funky
Dixieland and dance a honky-tonk,
And I'll be buyin' everybody drinks all 'round.
(To Chorus:)

BLINDED BY THE LIGHT

Bright rock ♩ = 138

Words and Music by
BRUCE SPRINGSTEEN

*Bass plays C pedal tone
throughout first chorus.

Vocal fades out until verse.

Blinded by the Light - 7 - 1

that's where the fun is.

Keybd.

D.S. % al Coda

3. Some

Coda

revved up like a deuce, an-oth-er run-ner in the night. Blind-

1. Mad-

-ed by the light, revved up like a deuce, an-oth-er

-man drum-mers, bum-mers, In-dians in the sum-mer with a teen-age dip-lo-mat.
with a sling-shot fi-n'lly found a ten-der spot and throws his lov-er in the sand.

run-ner in the night. Blind-ed by the light, revved up

In the dumps with the mumps as the ad-o-les-cent pumps his way
And some blood-shot for-get-me-not said, "Dad-dy's with-in ear-shot; save the

THE CHAIN

Gtr. tuned in Drop D:
⑥ = D ③ = G
⑤ = A ② = B
④ = D ① = E

Words and Music by
LINDSEY BUCKINGHAM, CHRISTINE McVIE,
STEVIE NICKS, MICK FLEETWOOD and JOHN McVIE

Moderately slow ♩ = 78

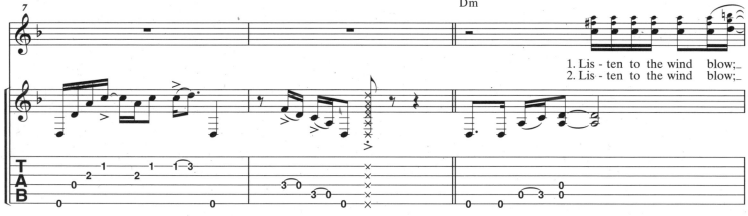

The Chain - 4 - 1

Run in the shad - ows,_____ damn your love; damn your lies._
Run in the shad - ows,_____ damn your love, damn your lies._

C6   B♭6

[1.   To Next Strain   [2.
Dm   (To Chorus:)   Dm

And if   Break the si - lence,_

C6   B♭6

Dm

damn the dark, damn_ the light._____   And if

Chorus:
Gm   Dm   B♭6

you don't love me now,__ you will nev-er love__ me a-gain. I can still hear you say - in' you would

The Chain - 4 - 2

40

The Chain - 4 - 4

CAN'T YOU HEAR ME KNOCKING

Elec. Gtr.1 in Open G tuning:
⑥ = D   ③ = G
⑤ = A   ② = B
④ = D   ① = D

Words and Music by
MICK JAGGER and KEITH RICHARDS

Moderately slow ♩ = 74

*Chord reflects overall tonality.

Verse 1:

Yeah,_ you got

Can't You Hear Me Knocking - 13 - 1

Can't You Hear Me Knocking - 13 - 2

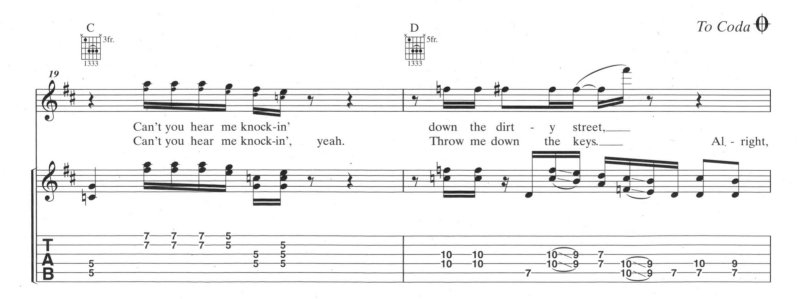

Coda

Chorus 2:
w/Rhy. Fig. 1 *(Elec. Gtr. 2) 8 times, simile*

.__now.   Hear me ring-ing,   big__ bells_ toll._

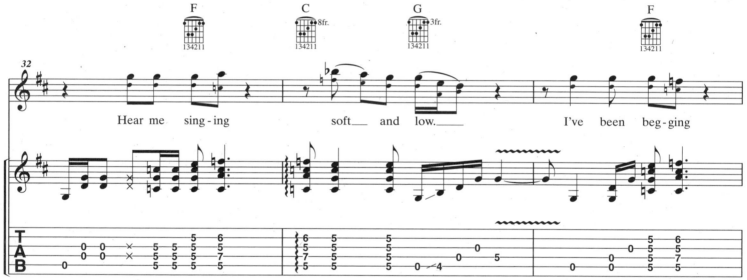

Hear me sing-ing   soft__ and low.__   I've been beg-ging

on__ my knees._   I've__ been kick-in',   help__ me please._

Hear me knock-in', I'm__ all, all a-round your town.__

Interlude:
Sax enters on repeat

*D7

Elec. Gtr. 1 *(clean-tone)*

* Chord reflects overall tonality.

Sax Solo:

Elec. Gtr. 1

Elec. Gtr. 2

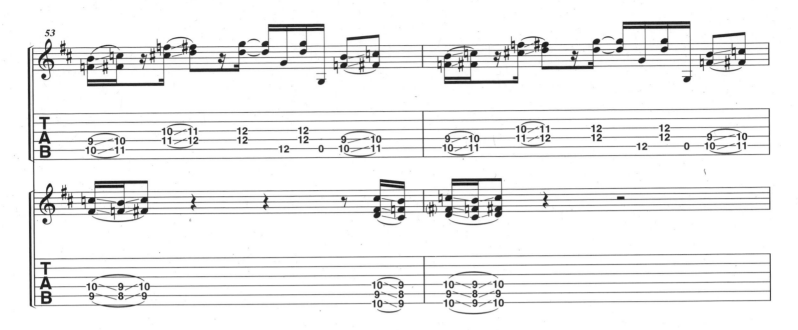

*Dm

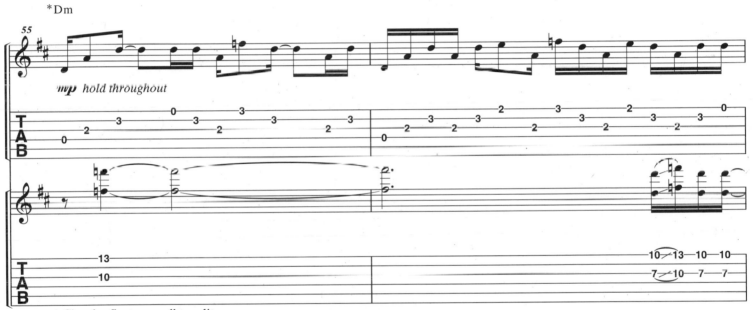

mp hold throughout

* Chord reflects overall tonality.

Can't You Hear Me Knocking - 13 - 8

Guitar Solo:

D5

Rhy. Fig. 2
Elec. Gtr. 1

end Rhy. Fig. 2

w/Rhy. Fig. 2 *(Elec. Gtr. 1) 10 times, simile*

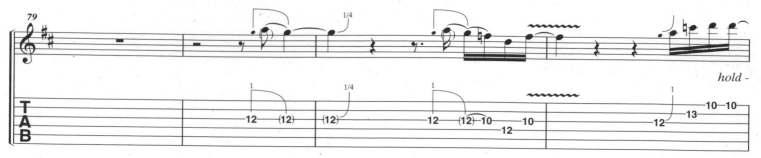

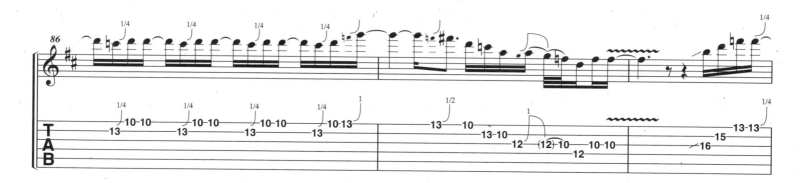

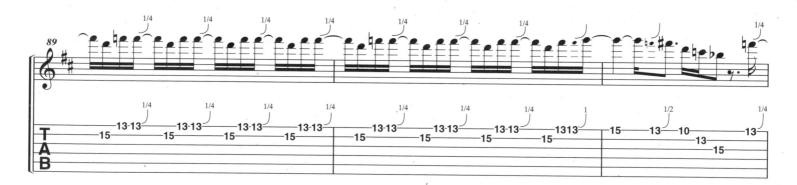

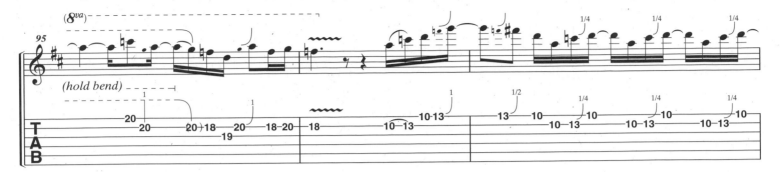

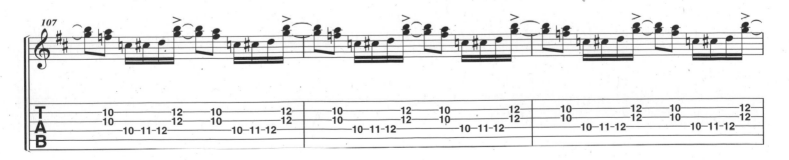

Can't You Hear Me Knocking - 13 - 12

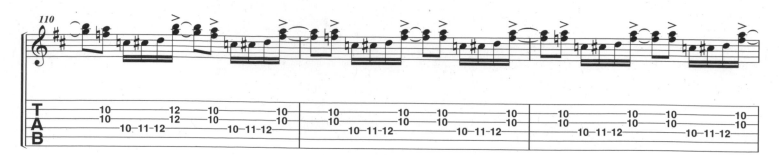

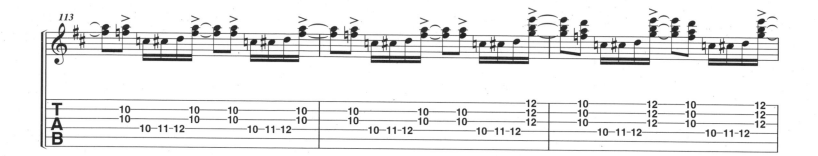

* Chord reflects overall tonality.

COMFORTABLY NUMB

Words and Music by
ROGER WATERS and DAVID GILMOUR

Moderately slow ♩ = 64

Come on, come on now,___ I hear you're feel-ing down.___ Well,
2. O-kay, o-kay,___ just a lit-tle pin-prick.___ There'll be no more,

Comfortably Numb - 7 - 1

56

58

Comfortably Numb - 7 - 4

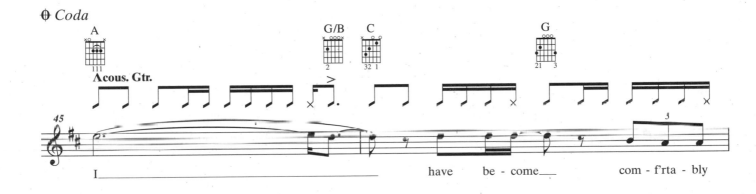

⊕ *Coda*

60   *Guitar Solo 2:*

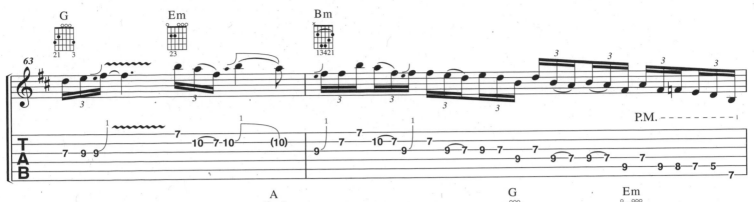

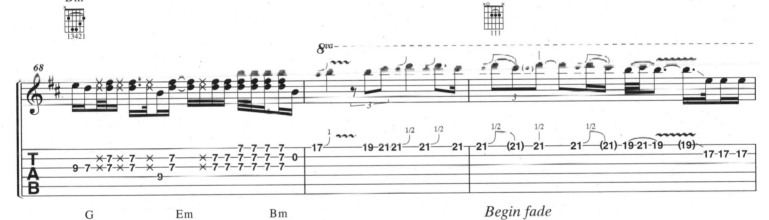

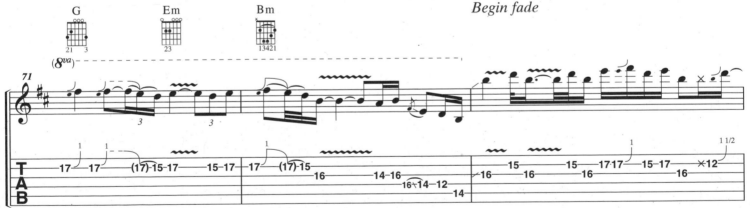

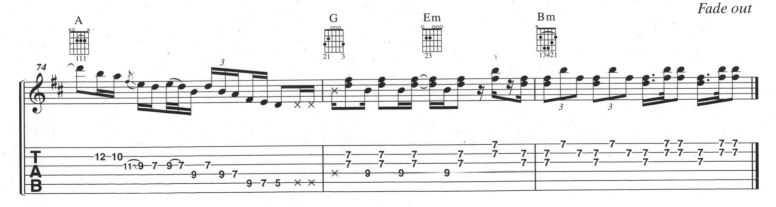

Comfortably Numb - 7 - 7

DEAR MR. FANTASY

Dear Mister Fan - ta - sy,___ play us a tune,___

some - thing to make___ us all___ hap - py.___

Do an - y - thing,___ take___ us out of this___ gloom.___ Sing a song,___

play gui - tar,___ make it snap - py.

Dear Mr. Fantasy - 6 - 1

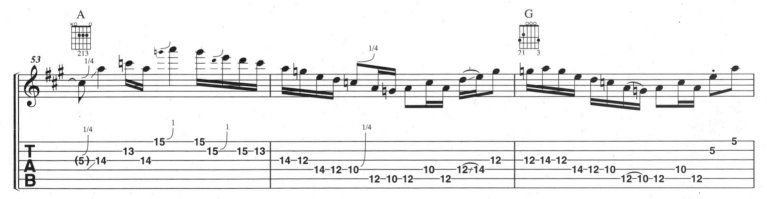

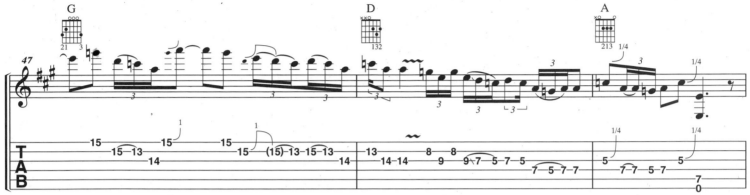

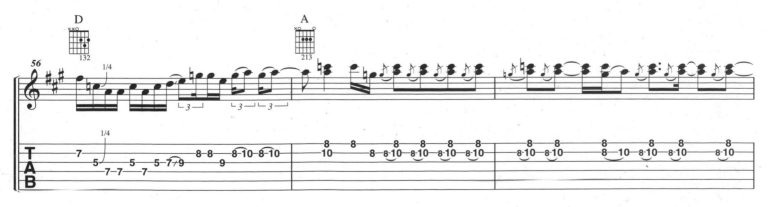

Dear Mr. Fantasy - 6 - 4

66

DO YOU FEEL LIKE WE DO

(live—radio edit)

Words and Music by
PETER FRAMPTON, JOHN SIOMOS,
RICK WILLIS and MICK GALLAGHER

Do You Feel Like We Do - 9 - 1

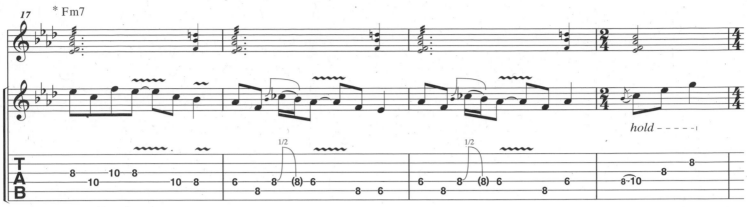

*Implied harmony.

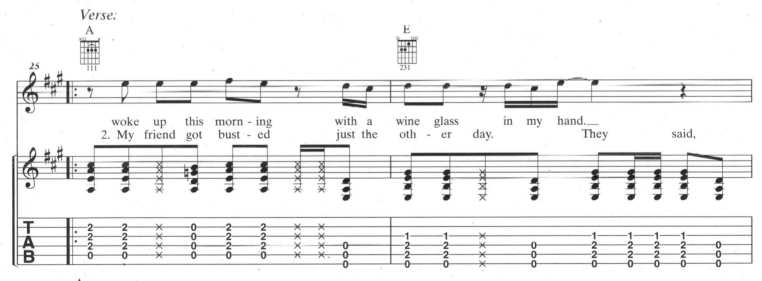

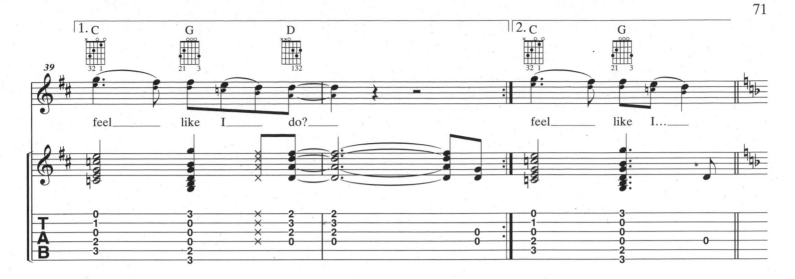

feel_____ like I_____ do?_____   feel_____ like I..._____

Guitar Solo:

Implied harmony.

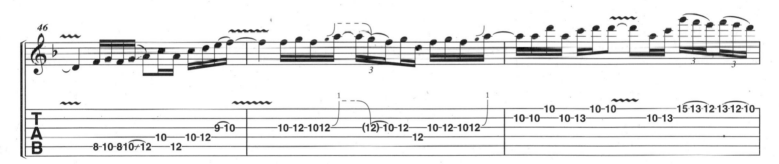

Do You Feel Like We Do - 9 - 4

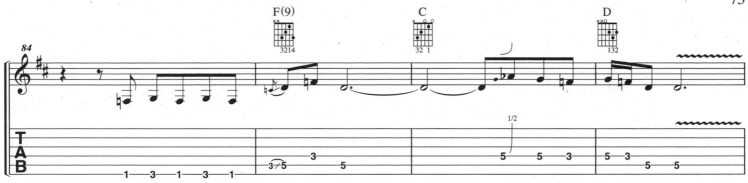

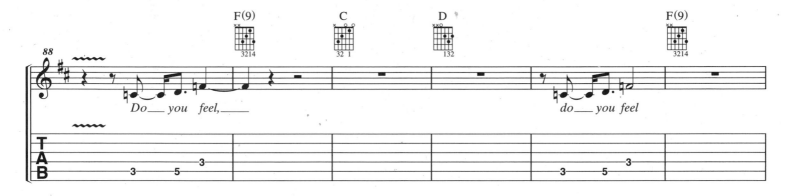

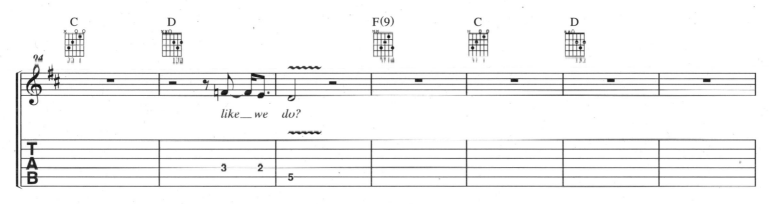

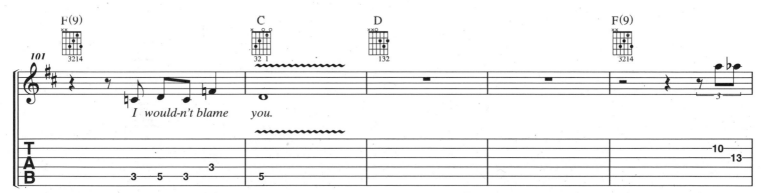

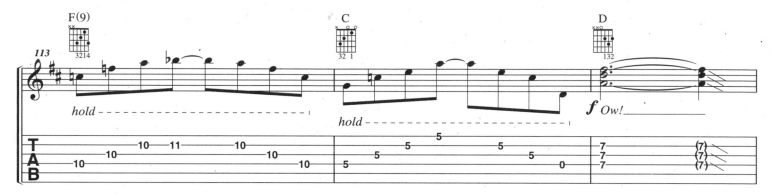

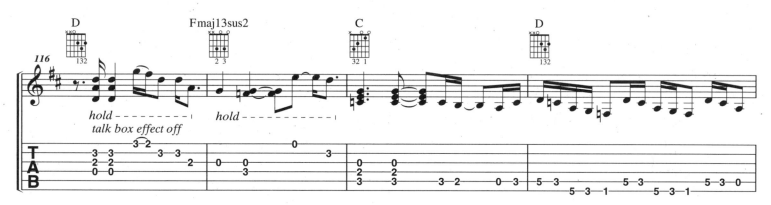

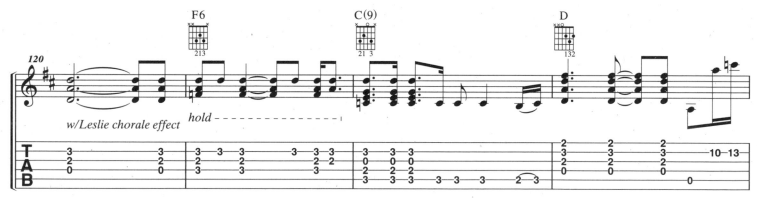

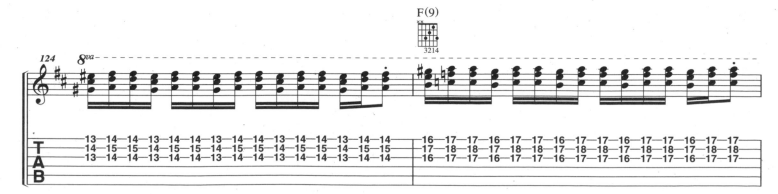

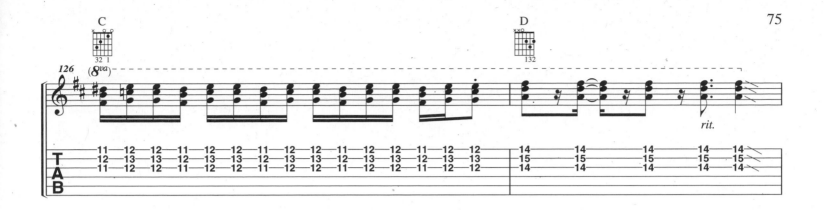

*Implied harmony.

Freely

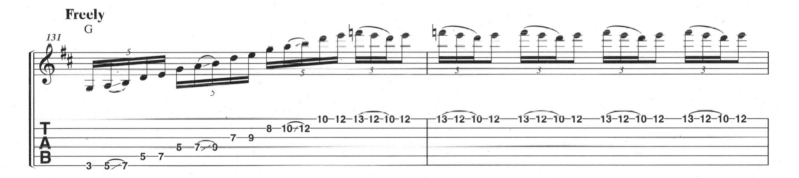

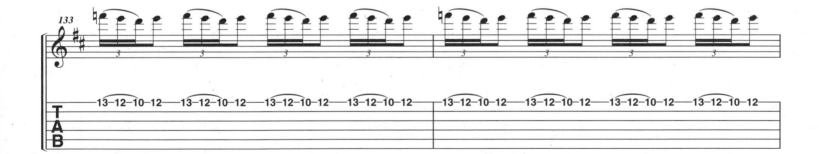

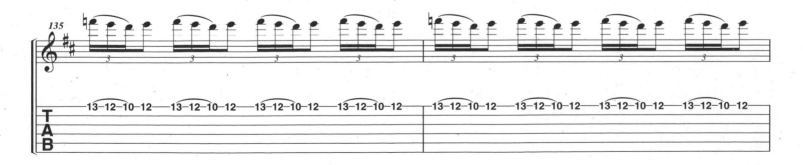

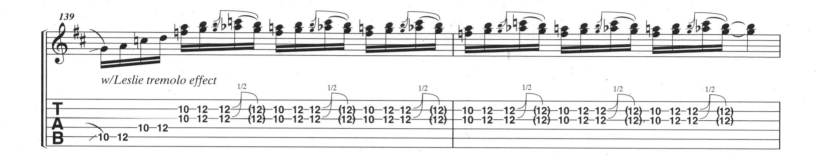

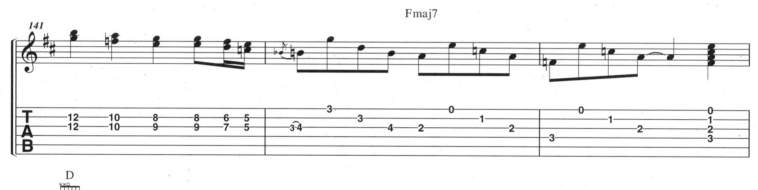

DOMINO

Words and Music by
VAN MORRISON

Moderately Fast ♩ = 130

Intro:

Gtr. 1

Verse:

1. Don't wan-na dis-cuss it,

think it's time for a change. ___

2. *See additional lyrics*

___ You may get dis-gust-ed,

Domino - 5 - 1

78

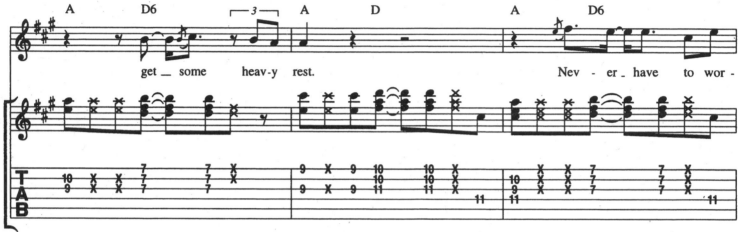

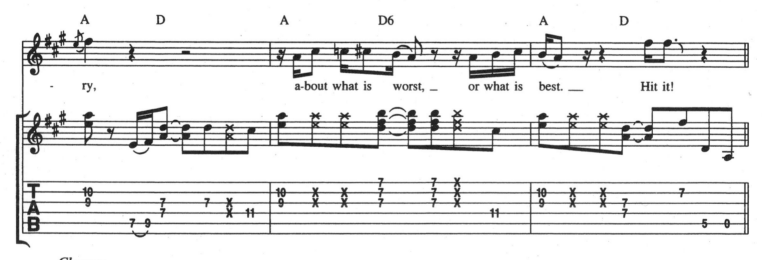

Chorus:

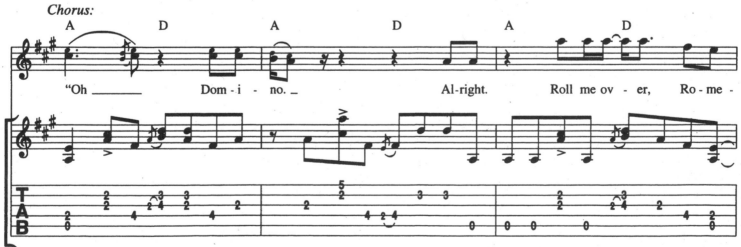

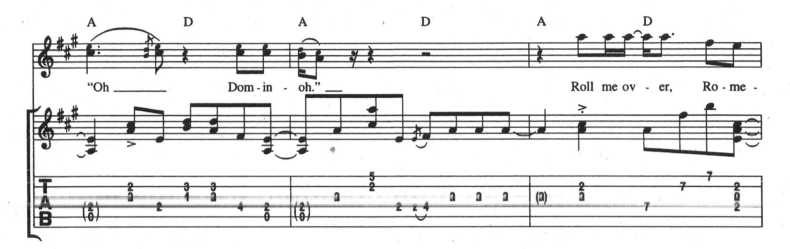

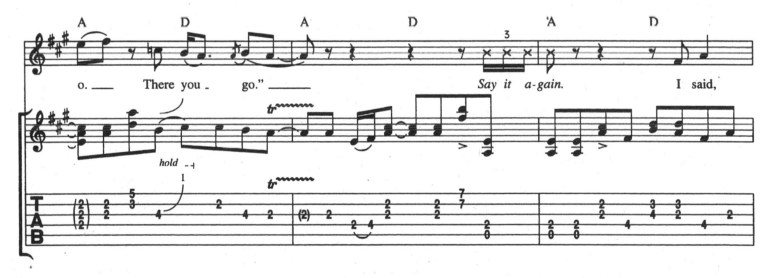

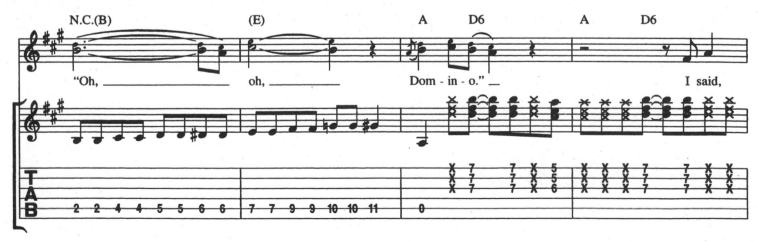

Domino - 5 - 3

"Oh, _____ oh, _____ Dom - in - o." ____

Dig it!
(2nd time) *Hey, Mr. D. J.,*

Horns:

I just wan-na hear some Rhy-thm and Blues mu - sic, _ yes. On the ra - di - o. On the ra - di - o. on the ra - di - o. Ah, a - a - al -

right. Ah, a - a - al - right. __ Ah, a - a - al - right. __ Ah ow. __ *Spoken: Hear the band.*

Outro:

Horns:

Verse 2:
There's no need for argument.
There's no argument at all.
And if you never hear from him,
That just means he didn't call.
Or vice-a-versa, that depends on wherever you're at.
Alright.
And if you never hear from me, that just means I would rather not.
(To Chorus:)

DON'T STOP 'TIL YOU GET ENOUGH

Moderately ♩ = 102

Written and Composed by
MICHAEL JACKSON

(Spoken:) You know I was, I was wondering, you know, that if we should keep on, because the force, it,

it's got a lot of power, and you make me feel like, you make me feel like... ooh.

Don't Stop 'Til You Get Enough - 5 - 1

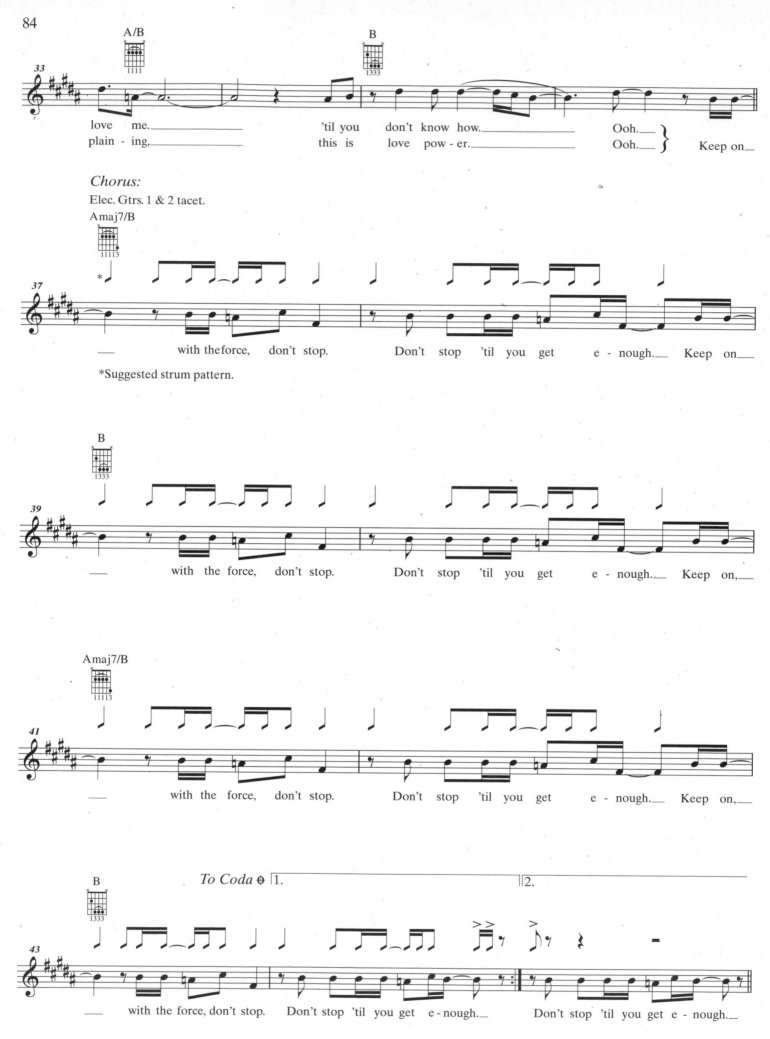

Verse 4:

w/Rhy. Figs. 1 *(Elec. Gtr. 2)* **& 1A** *(Elec. Gtr. 1), both 2 times*

Love - ly_____ is the feel - ing____ now._____ I won't_ be com-

plain - ing,____ the force is love pow - er._____ Ooh.__ Keep on,__

Chorus:

w/Rhy. Figs. 1 *(Elec. Gtr. 2)* **& 1A** *(Elec. Gtr. 1), both 2 times*

Amaj7/B

Resume chorus fig. simile

__ with the force, don't stop. Don't stop 'til you get e - nough.__ Keep on__

__ with the force, don't stop. Don't stop 'til you get e - nough.__ Keep on,__

__ with the force, don't stop. Don't stop 'til you get e - nough.__ Keep on,__

Repeat ad lib. and fade

__ with the force, don't stop. Don't stop 'til you get e - nough. Keep on,__

Verse 3:
Heratbreak, enemy despise.
Eternal love shines in my eyes.
Ooh, so let love take us through the hours.
I won't be complaining.
Your love is all mine. Ooh.
(To Chorus:)

EUROPA (EARTH'S CRY HEAVEN' SMILE)

Words and Music by
CARLOS SANTANA and TOM COSTER

Europa (Earth's Cry Heaven's Smile) - 7 - 1

90

Europa (Earth's Cry Heaven's Smile) - 7 - 5

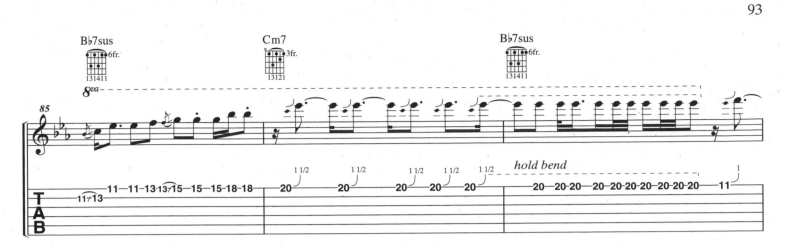

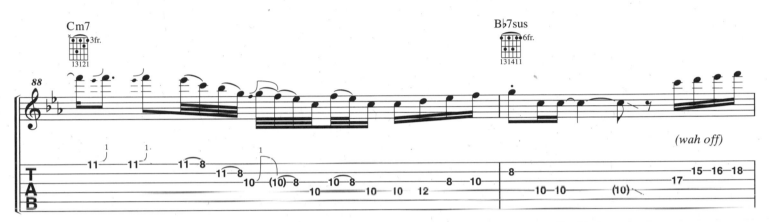

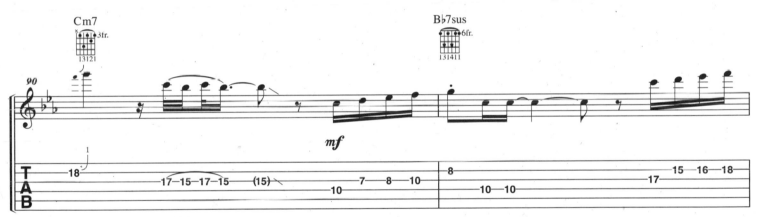

Europa (Earth's Cry Heaven's Smile) - 7 - 7

ERUPTION

By EDWARD VAN HALEN, ALEX VAN HALEN,
MICHAEL ANTHONY and DAVID LEE ROTH

*w/slight flanging and tape echo delay.

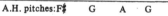

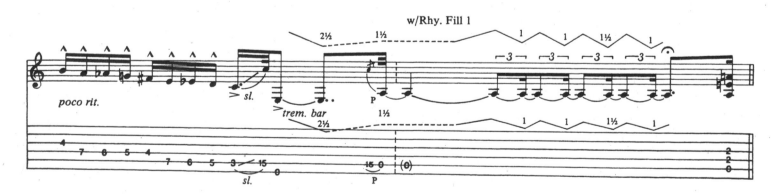

Eruption - 4 - 1

*Release finger pressure when arriving at 19fr. at end
of slide to sound F# natural harmonic.

Faster (♩ = 132)

Rhy. Fill 1

Overdubbed gtr.

*w/more intense flanging.

*w/flanger (slow sweep, medium intensity & regeneration)
& tape echo delay (approx. 150 ms. w/one repeat).

(A)
(A dim)
(B)

*Slightly rushed.

97

*Slightly rushed.

*Tap open low E at 12fr.
to produce octave harmonic.

Fdbk. pitch: B

**Univox tape echo runaway feedback effect.

Eruption - 4 - 4

EVERY PICTURE TELLS A STORY

Drop D tuning: ⑥ = D

Moderately fast ♩ = 140

Intro:

Words and Music by
ROD STEWART and RON WOOD

© 1971 (Renewed) WARNER-TAMERLANE PUBLISHING CORP., UNICHAPPELL MUSIC INC.
and EMI BLACKWOOD MUSIC, INC.
All Rights Reserved

Every Picture Tells a Story - 6 - 1

Bridge:

mem - ber, ev - 'ry pic - ture tells a sto - ry, don't___ it?

Outro:

D

Ev - 'ry pic - ture tells a sto - ry, don't___ it?

Acous. & Elec. Gtrs.

Repeat ad lib. and fade

Ev - 'ry pic - ture tells a sto - ry, don't it?

Verse 2:
Paris was a place you could hide away
If you felt you didn't fit in.
French police wouldn't give me no peace,
They claimed I was a nasty person.
Down along the Left Bank minding my own, whoo,
Was knocked down by a human stampede.
Got arrested for inciting a peaceful riot
When all I wanted was a cup of tea.
I was accused, whoo!
I moved on.

Verse 3:
Down in Rome I wasn't getting enough
Of the things that keep a young man alive.
My body stunk but I kept my funk, whoo,
At a time when I was right out of luck.
Getting desperate, indeed I was, yeah,
Looking like a tourist attraction.
Oh, my dear, I better get out of here
For the Vatican don't give no sanction.
I wasn't ready for that, no, no.
I moved right out east, yeah! Listen...

Verse 4:
On the Peking ferry I was feeling merry
Sailing on my way back here.
I fell in love with a slit-eyed lady
By the light of an eastern moon.
Shanghai Lil never used the pill,
She claimed that it just ain't natural.
She took me up on deck and bit my neck,
Oh, people, I was glad I found her.
Oh yeah, I was glad I found her. Whoo, hoo!
(To Bridge:)

Verse 5:
The women I've known I wouldn't let tie my shoe,
They wouldn't give you the time of day.
But the slit-eyed lady knocked me off my feet,
God, I was glad I found her.
And if they had the words, I could tell to you
To help you on the way down the road.
I couldn't quote you no Dickens, Shelley or Keats
'Cause it's all been said before.
Make the best out of the bad just laugh it off, ha,
You didn't have to come here anyway.
(To Outro:)

Every Picture Tells a Story - 6 - 6

FAMILY AFFAIR

Words and Music by
SYLVESTER STEWART

Family Affair - 4 - 1

Instrumental:

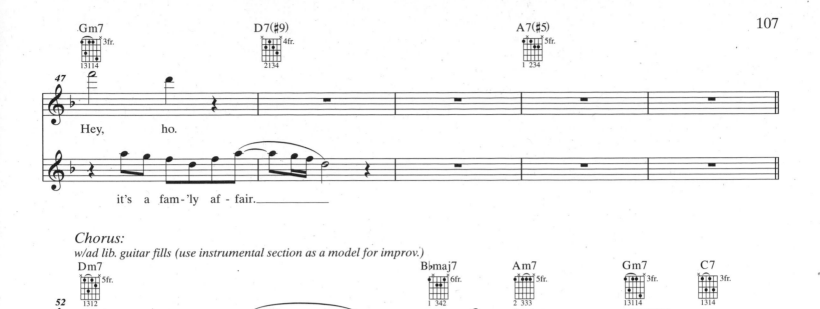

Chorus:
w/ad lib. guitar fills (use instrumental section as a model for improv.)

It's a fam-'ly af-fair,_____

It's a fam-'ly af-fair,_____

It's a fam-'ly af-fair,_____

It's a fam-'ly af-fair,_____

Outro: *Repeat and fade*

Verse 2:
Newlywed a year ago
But you're still checking each other out, hey, hey.
Nobody wants to blow,
Nobody wants to be left out.
You can't leave, 'cause your heart is there.
But you can't stay, 'cause you been somewhere else.
You can't cry, 'cause you'll look broke down.
But you're cryin' anyway 'cause you're all broke down.
It's a family affair…
(To Coda)

FRIDAY ON MY MIND

Words and Music by
GEORGE VANDA and HARRY VANDA

112

Friday on My Mind - 5 - 5

HELLO MARY LOU (GOODBYE HEART)

Words and Music by
GENE PITNEY and CAYET MANGIARACINA

Hello Mary Lou (Goodbye Heart) - 5 - 3

Lyrics:
I knew, Ma - ry Lou,___ we'd nev - er part.___ So hel - lo,___ Ma - ry Lou,___ good - bye___ heart.

To Coda

Guitar Solo:
Cont. rhy. simile

Elec. Gtr.

f fingerstyle

D.S. al Coda

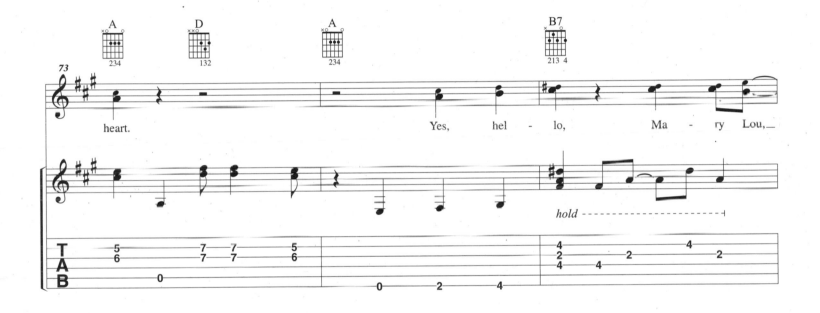

I PUT A SPELL ON YOU

Words and Music by
JAY HAWKINS

Cont. in slashes

I Put a Spell on You - 7 - 4

122

*Apply very fast vibrato w/trem. bar while bending note with left hand.

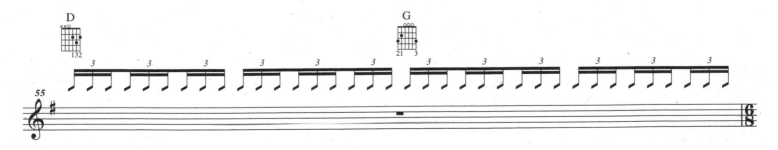

I Put a Spell on You - 7 - 6

I DON'T NEED NO DOCTOR

Words and Music by
NICKOLAS ASHFORD, VALERIE SIMPSON
and JOSIE ARMSTEAD

I Don't Need No Doctor - 9 - 5

(4:06)

Guitar Solo 3:

Elec. Gtr. 2

Rhy. Fig. 2 - - - - - - - - - - - - - - - - -

Elec. Gtr. 1

I Don't Need No Doctor - 9 - 7

132

I Don't Need No Doctor - 9 - 9

ITCHYCOO PARK

Words and Music by
STEVE MARIOTT and RONALD LANE

Itchycoo Park - 4 - 1

Chorus:

Outro:

Repeat and fade

Itchycoo Park - 4 - 4

LAY DOWN SALLY

*Chord frames are for reference.

%. *Verse:*

1.There is noth - ing that___ is wrong___ in want-ing you___ to stay___
2.3.*See additional lyrics*

Elec. Gtr. 1

Elec. Gtr. 2

___ here___ with me.   I

141

Lay Down Sally - 8 - 4

D.S. % al Coda

3. I

Verse 2:
The sun ain't nearly on the rise,
And we still got the moon and stars above.
Underneath the velvet skies,
Love is all that matters; won't you stay with me?
And don't you ever leave.
(To Chorus:)

Verse 3:
I long to see the morning light
Coloring your face so dreamily.
So, don't you go and say goodbye;
You can lay your worries down and stay with me,
And don't you ever leave.
(To Chorus:)

Lay Down Sally - 8 - 8

LAYLA

Words and Music by
ERIC CLAPTON and JIM GORDON

Moderately ♩ = 117

w/Riff A (Elec. Gtr. 1) 4 times

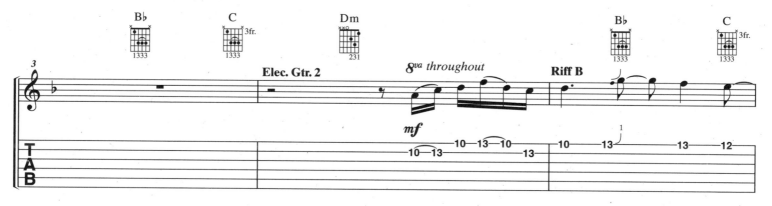

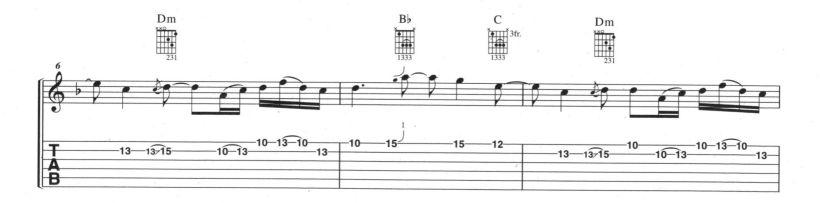

Layla - 6 - 1

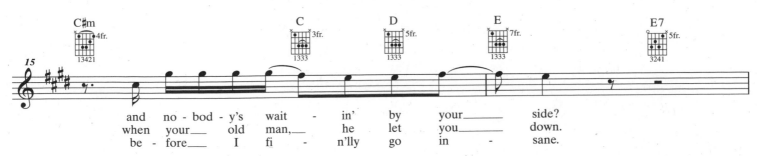

148

Layla - 6 - 3

Coda I

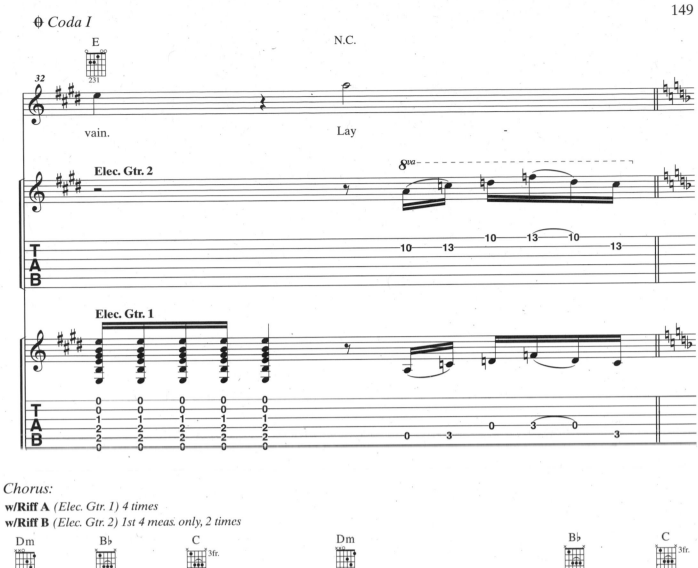

Chorus:

w/Riff A *(Elec. Gtr. 1) 4 times*
w/Riff B *(Elec. Gtr. 2) 1st 4 meas. only, 2 times*

la,_____ you got me on__ my knees.__ Lay - la,_____ I

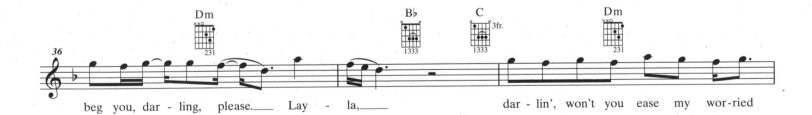

beg you, dar - ling, please.__ Lay - la,_____ dar - lin', won't you ease my wor-ried

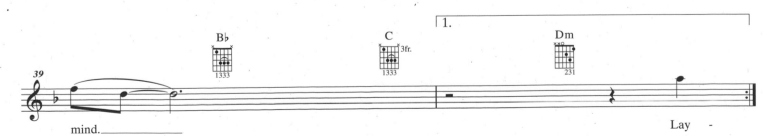

mind._____ Lay -

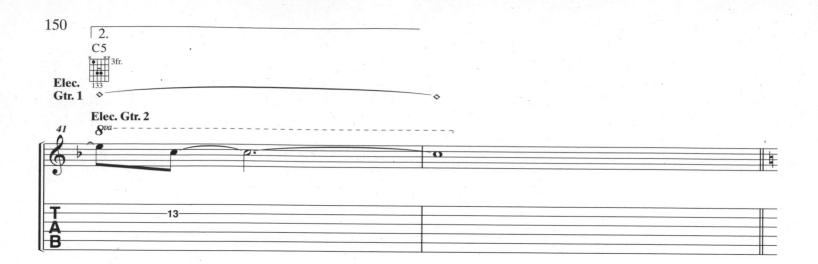

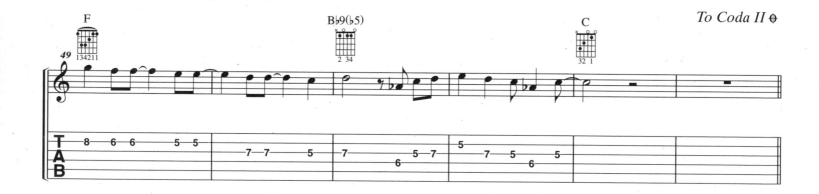

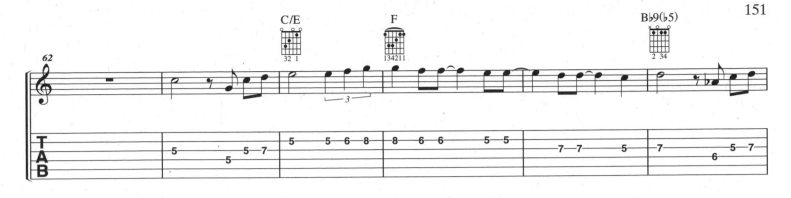

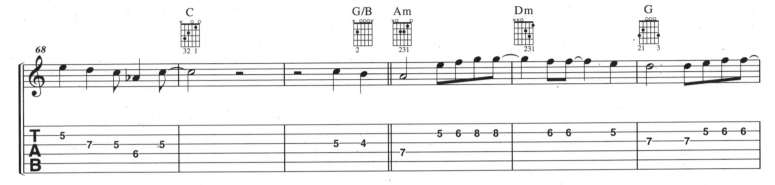

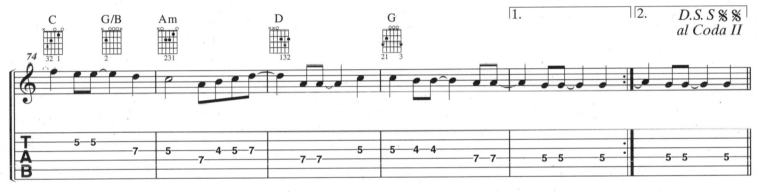

Coda II

I THANK YOU

Words and Music by
DAVID PORTER and ISAAC HAYES

Verse lyrics:

did-n't have to love___ me like you did, but you did, but you did, and I
(2.) did-n't have to squeeze___ but you did, but you did, but you did, and I
(3.) did-n't have to shake___ it but you did, but you did, but you did, and I

*Elec. Gtr. 1 is a composite arrangement.

I Thank You - 5 - 1

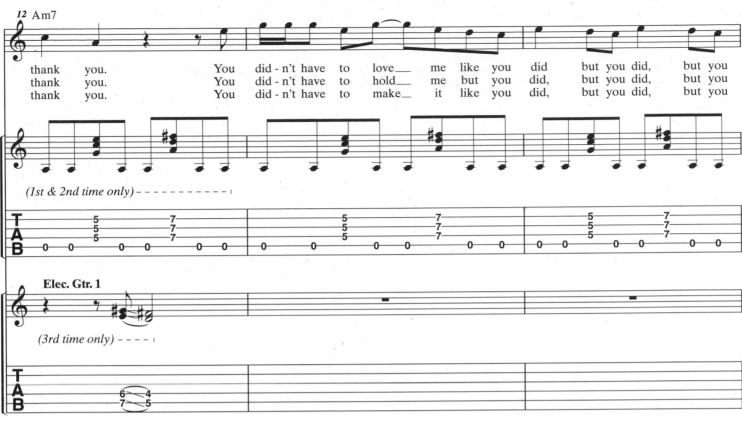

Coda

Outro:

thank you.

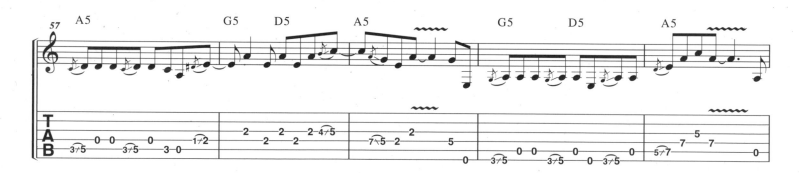

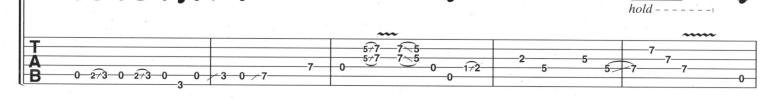

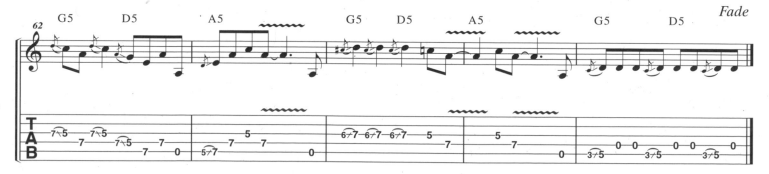

Begin Fade

Fade

hold - - - - - - -|

LIGHTS

Words and Music by
NEAL SCHON and STEVE PERRY

Lights - 7 - 1

158

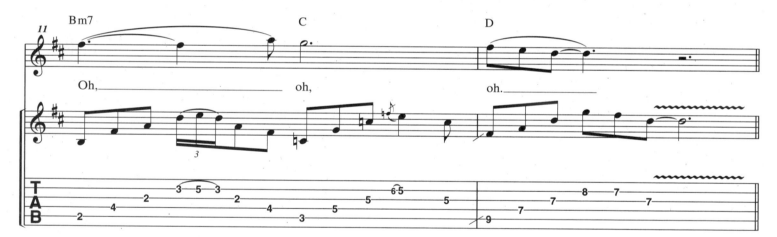

Verse:

Lights - 7 - 2

Lights - 7 - 3

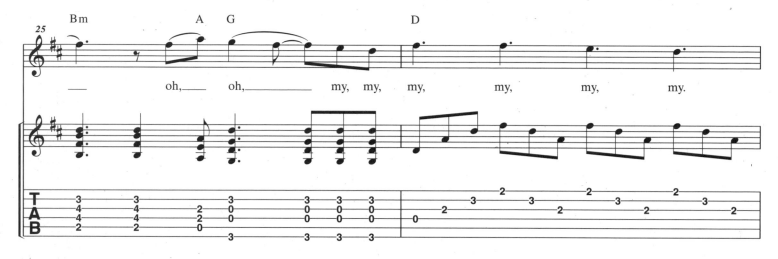

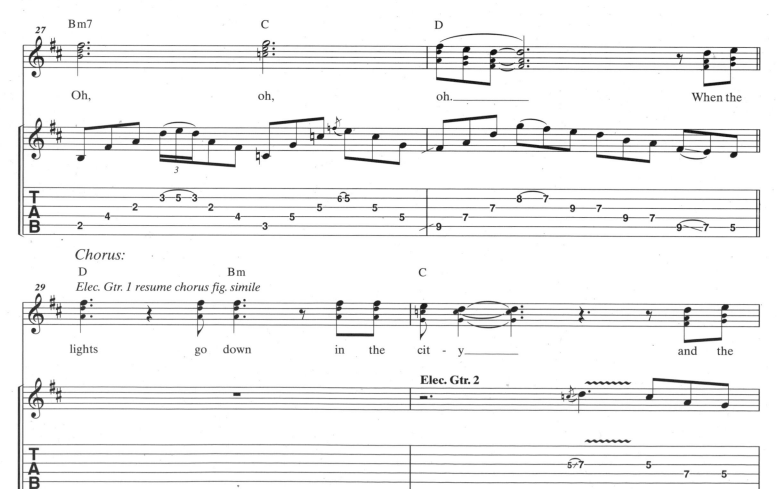

Chorus:

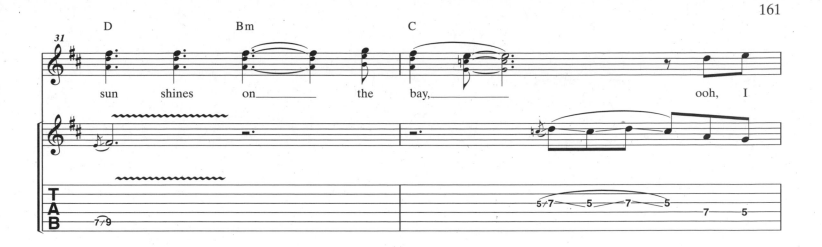

sun   shines   on_____   the   bay,_____   ooh,   I

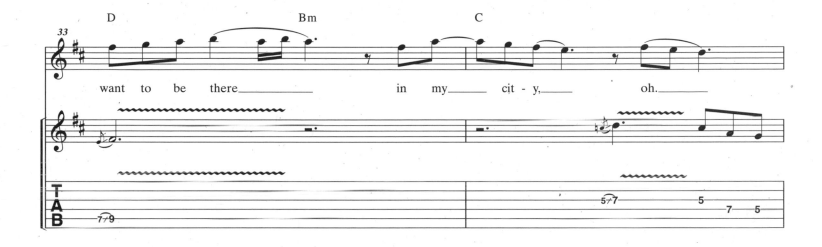

want   to   be   there_____   in   my_____   cit - y,_____   oh._____

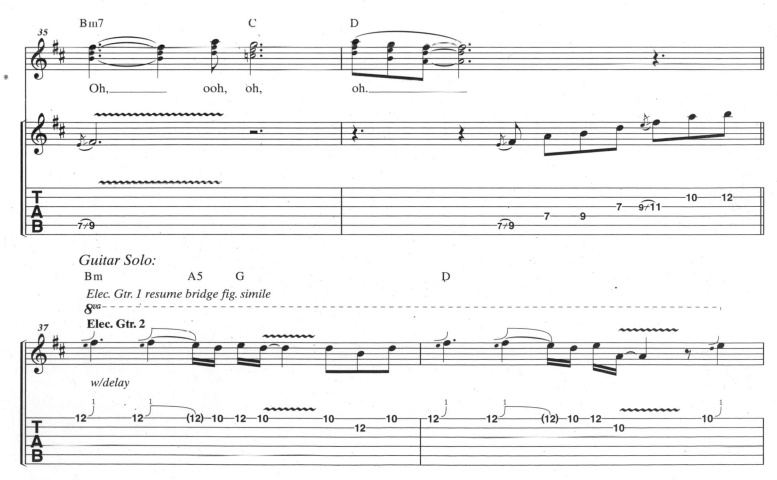

Oh,_____   ooh,   oh,   oh.

Guitar Solo:

Bm   A5   G   D

Elec. Gtr. 1 resume bridge fig. simile

Elec. Gtr. 2

w/delay

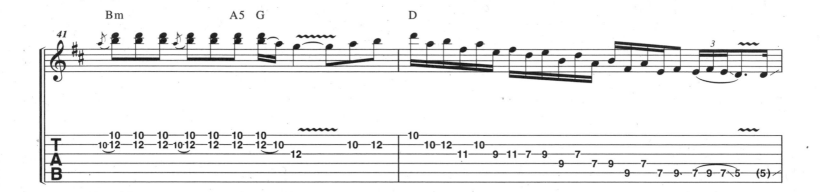

Chorus:

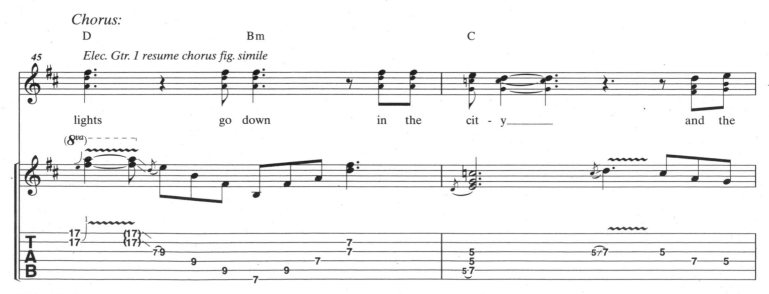

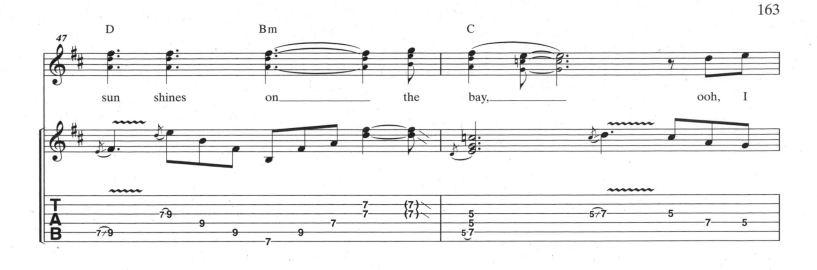

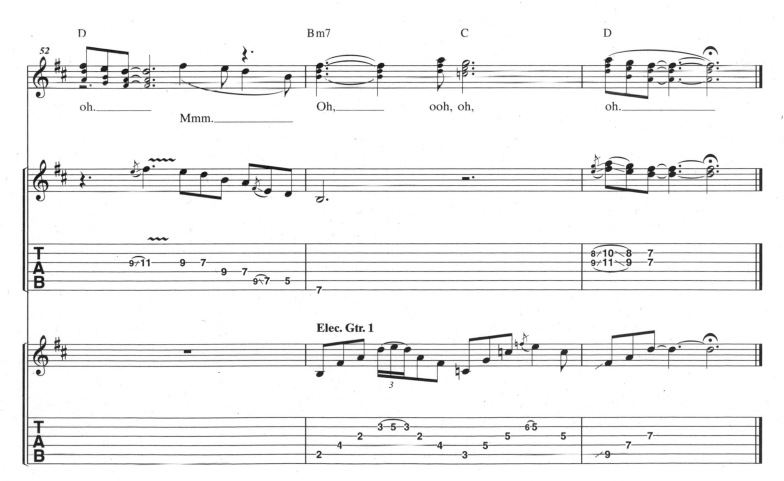

MIDNIGHT RIDER

Words and Music by
ROBERT PAYNE and GREGG ALLMAN

Guitar Solo:
w/Rhy. Fig. 1 *(Acous. Gtr.) simile*

MRS. ROBINSON

To match record key, Capo II

Words and Music by
PAUL SIMON

Moderately bright ♩ = 104

Intro:

Dee   dee dee dee   dee   dee   dee dee   dee   dee   dee dee   dee.___

Do   do do do   do   do   do do do.___

Mrs. Robinson - 4 - 1

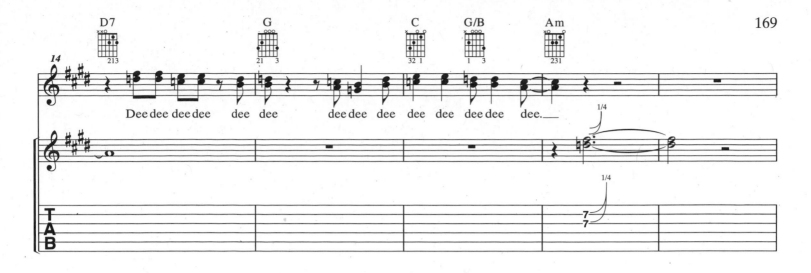

Mrs. Robinson - 4 - 2

Mrs. Robinson - 4 - 4

ONE

(as recorded by Three Dog Night)

Moderate shuffle ♩ = 126

Words and Music by
HARRY NILSSON

One - 5 - 1

Verse 2:

No is the sad - dest ex - pe - ri-ence you'll ev - er know.

mp

w/volume swells

Yes, it's the sad - dest ex - pe - ri-ence you'll ev - er know. 'Cause

loco

one is the lone - li-est num - ber_____ that you'll ev - er do._____

Rhy. Fig. 1

end Rhy. Fig. 1 One is the lone - li-est num - ber,_____ oh,_____

One - 5 - 2

worse than two.___

Bridge 1: *Rhythm out*
(Piano plays quarter-note chords, as intro)

It's just no good an-y-more__ since she went a-way._____ Now I

spend my time__ just mak-ing rhymes of yes-ter-day._____ **Drums**

w/volume swells

Chorus:
w/Rhy. Fig. 1 *(Elec. Gtr.) cont. simile, 2 times*

One is the lone-li-est__ num-ber,__ one__ is the lone-li-est num-ber, one__

__ is the lone-li-est num-ber that you'll ev-er do.__

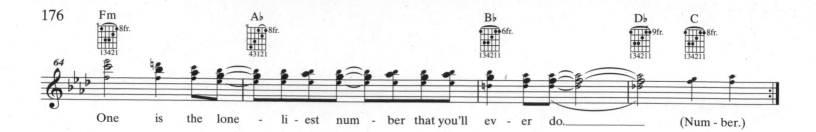

One is the lone - li - est num - ber that you'll ev - er do._____ (Num - ber.)

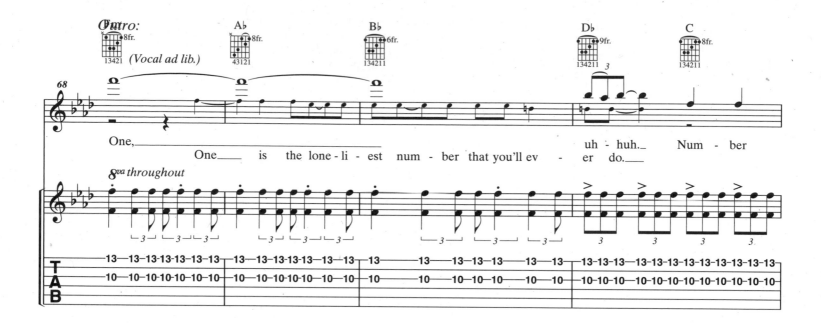

Outro:

(Vocal ad lib.)

One,_____ One____ is the lone - li - est num - ber that you'll ev - er do.__ uh - huh.__ Num - ber

8va throughout

w/Rhy. Fig. 1 *(Elec. Gtr.) cont. simile, 2 times*

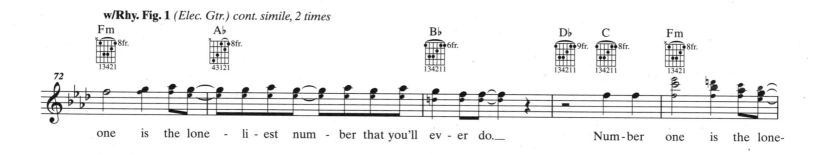

one is the lone - li - est num - ber that you'll ev - er do.__ Num - ber one is the lone-

loco

- li - est num - ber that you'll ev - er do._____

ONE OF THESE NIGHTS

Words and Music by
DON HENLEY and GLENN FREY

*Elec. Gtr. 1 is a composite arrangement.

*Elec. Gtr. 2 is two guitars arr. for one.

One of These Nights - 7 - 1

*Two gtrs. arr. for one.

One of These Nights - 7 - 3

*Two gtrs. arr. for one.

One of These Nights - 7 - 7

RIDE MY SEE-SAW

Words and Music by
JOHN LODGE

186

Ride My See-Saw - 4 - 3

RIGHT PLACE, WRONG TIME

Moderately ♩ = 104

Words and Music by
MAC REBENNACK

Right Place, Wrong Time - 4 - 4

ROCK AND ROLL ALL NITE

Words and Music by
PAUL STANLEY and GENE SIMMONS

*All gtrs. tuned down 1/2 step:
⑥ = E♭ ③ = G♭
⑤ = A♭ ② = B♭
④ = D♭ ① = E♭

Moderately ♩ = 142

*Recording sounds a half step lower than written.

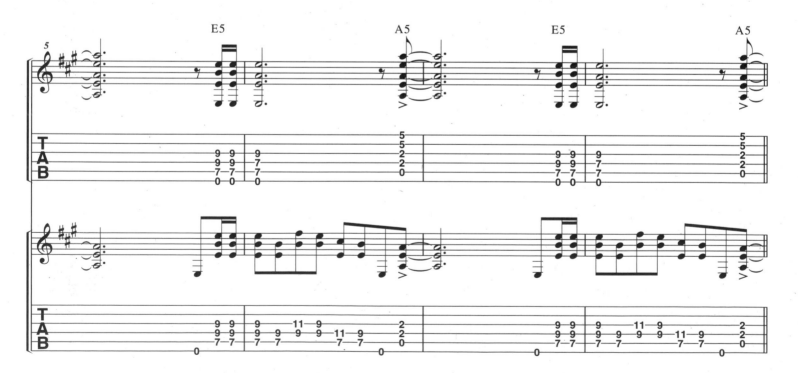

Rock and Roll All Nite - 8 - 1

Verse:

1. You show us ev - 'ry - thing you've got,_____
2. You keep on say - ing you'll be mine for a while,_____

you keep on danc - ing and the room gets hot.
you're look - ing fan - cy and I like your style.

Pre-chorus:

You keep on shout - ing, you_____ keep on shout - ing.

Come on!_____

I_____

𝄋 *Chorus:*

wan - na rock and roll_____ all night,_____

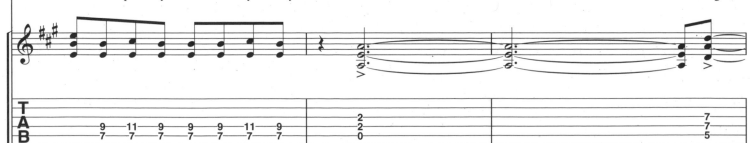

and par - ty e - ver - y day._____ I wan - na rock and roll_____ all night,_____

Elec. Gtrs. 1 & 2 tacet 6 meas.

To Coda

198

Guitar Solo:

Rock and Roll All Nite - 8 - 7

(WE'RE GONNA) ROCK AROUND THE CLOCK

Words and Music by
MAX C. FREEDMAN
and JIMMY DE KNIGHT

(We're Gonna) Rock Around the Clock - 4 - 1

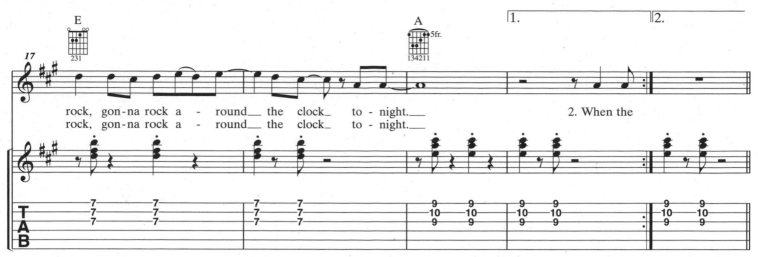

rock, gon-na rock a - round__ the clock__ to - night.__
rock, gon-na rock a - round__ the clock__ to - night.__

2. When the

Guitar Solo:

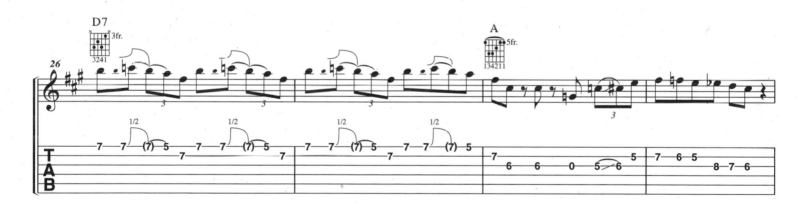

3. When the

(We're Gonna) Rock Around the Clock - 4 - 2

(We're Gonna) Rock Around the Clock - 4 - 4

ROUNDABOUT

Words and Music by
JON ANDERSON and STEVE HOWE

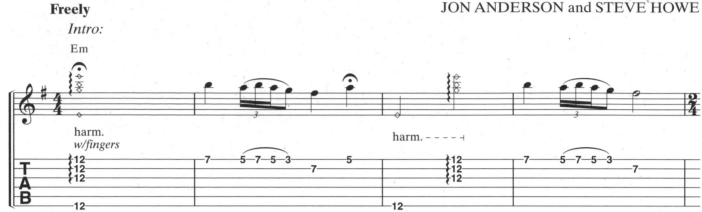

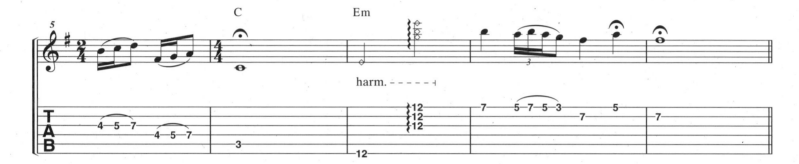

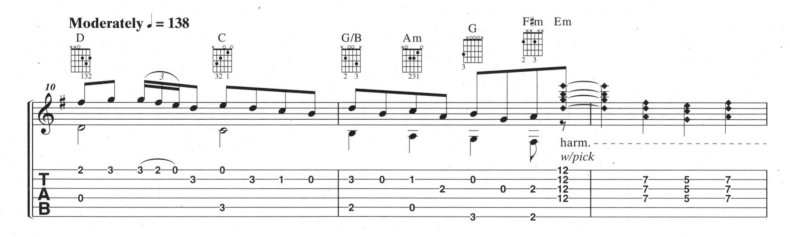

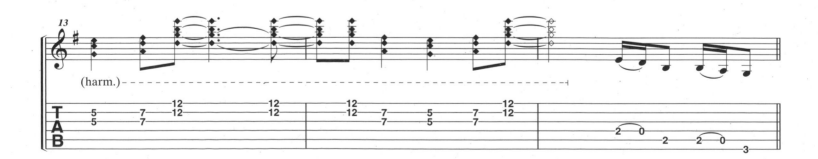

Roundabout - 6 - 1

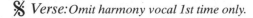

§ *Verse:Omit harmony vocal 1st time only.*

w/Rhy. Fig. 1 *(on repeats) cont. simile, 3 times*

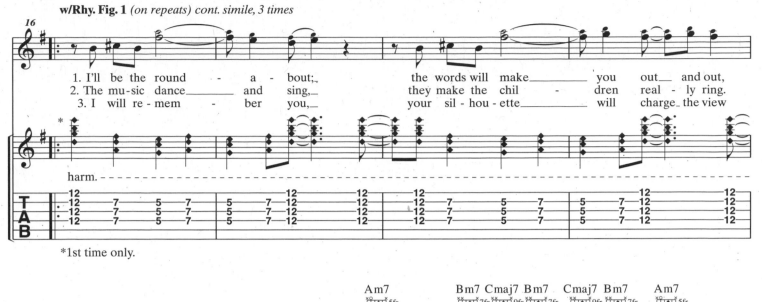

1. I'll be the round - a - bout;___ the words will make____ you out_ and out,
2. The mu-sic dance____ and sing,_ they make the chil - dren real - ly ring.
3. I will re - mem - ber you,_ your sil - hou - ette____ will charge_ the view

harm. - - - - - - - - - - - - - - -

*1st time only.

I'll spend the day_____ your way._____
I spend the day_____ your way._____
of dis - tant at - mo - sphere.

(harm.) -

Call it

Cont. in slashes

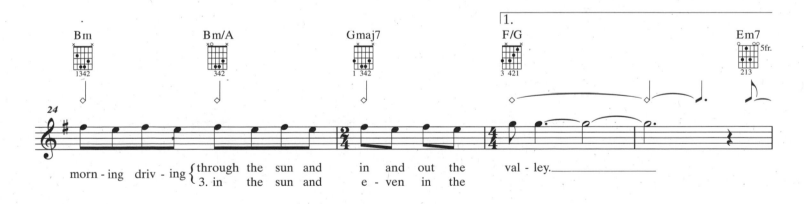

morn - ing driv - ing { through the sun and in and out the val - ley.____
3. in the sun and e - ven in the

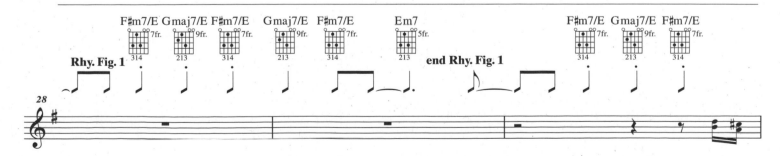

Rhy. Fig. 1

end Rhy. Fig. 1

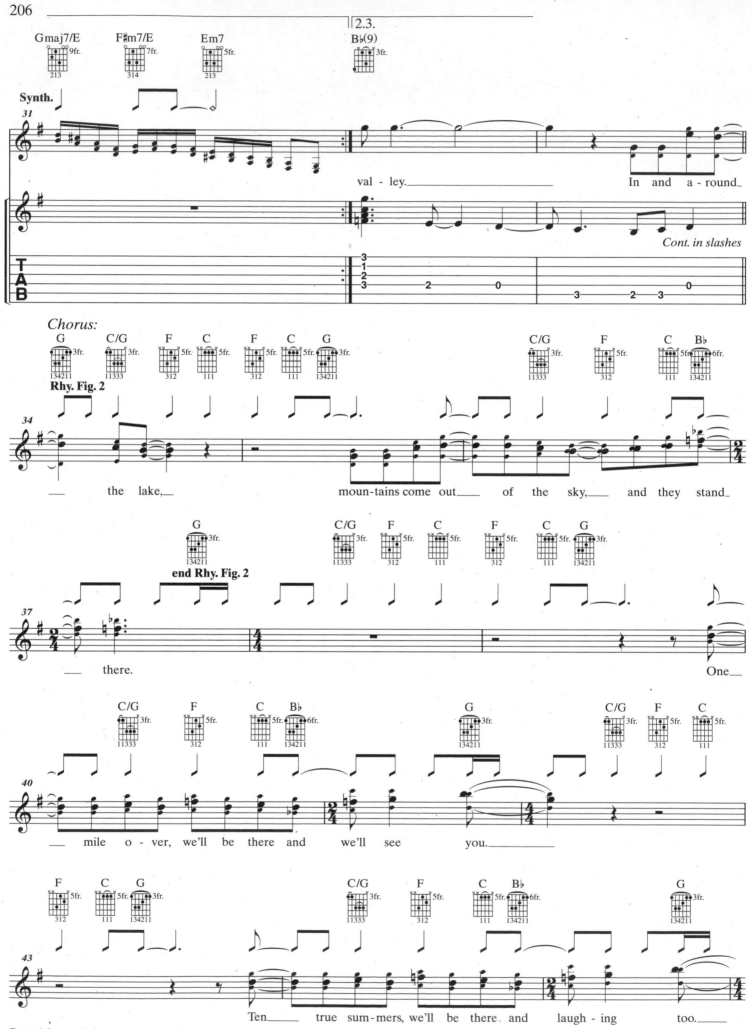

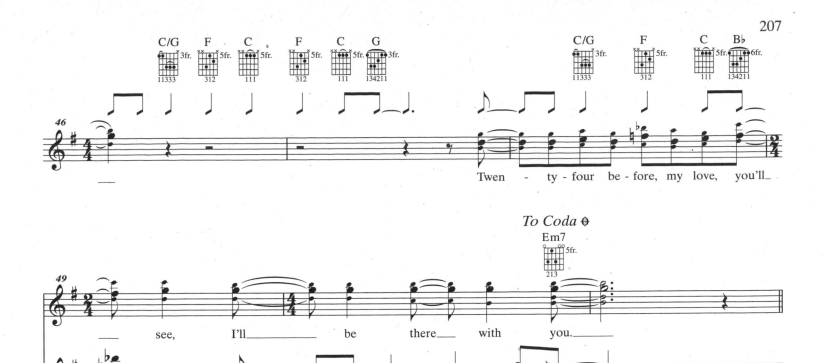

Twen - ty-four be - fore, my love, you'll

To Coda

see, I'll____ be there____ with you.____

w/fingers

Organ Solo:

Play 4 times

w/pick

*Legato slurs for easy arrangement.
Individual notes are picked on recording.

208

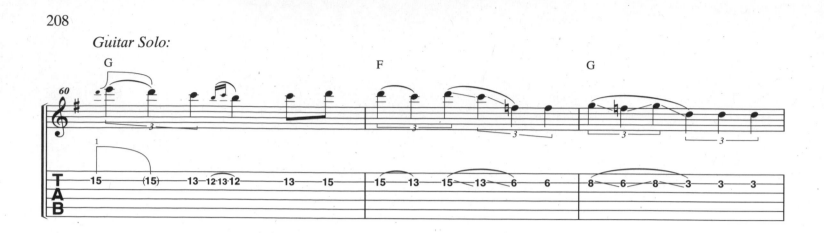

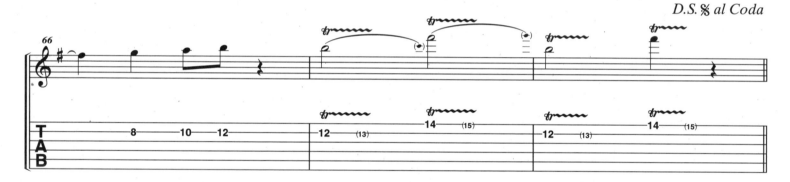

Roundabout - 6 - 5

RUNNING ON EMPTY

Words and Music by
JACKSON BROWNE

Running on Empty - 8 - 1

214

Verse 4:
w/Rhy. Figs. 1(*Elec. Gtr. 1*) **& 1A** (*Elec. Gtr. 2*) *both 2 times, simile*

Hon - ey, you real - ly tempt___ me,____ you know the way you look___ so kind.___

I'd love to stick a - round_____ but I'm run - ning be - hind.___

You know I don't e - ven know___ what I'm hop - ing to find.___

Run - ning on._____

Run - ning dry._____ Run - ning in - to the sun___

216

but I'm run-ning be-hind.

pick slide

Outro:
w/Rhy. Fig. 1 *(Elec. Gtr. 1) 12 times, simile*

Lap Steel Gtr.

Elec. Gtr. 2

Lap Steel Gtr.
8va throughout

Verse 2:
Gotta do what you can just to keep your love alive.
Tryin' not to confuse and with what you do to survive.
Sixty-nine, I was twenty-one, and I called the road my own.
I don't know when that road turned on to be the road I'm on.
(To Chorus:)

Verse 3:
Looking out at the road rushing under my wheels.
I don't know how to tell you all just how crazy this life feels.
I look around for the friends that I used to turn to, to pull me through.
Looking into their eyes, I see them running too.
(To Chorus:)

Running on Empty - 8 - 8

SHAPES OF THINGS

Words and Music by
PAUL SAMWELL-SMITH,
JAMES McCARTY and KEITH RELF

Shapes of Things - 5 - 1

Shapes of Things - 5 - 2

SHOOTING STAR

Words and Music by
PAUL RODGERS

*Acous. Gtrs. 1 & 2, & Elec. Gtr. 1 in Open A tuning.
Elec. Gtrs. 2 (Chorus and Guitar Solo) & 3 (Guitar Solo and fills), both entering at measure 12, are in standard tuning.
**Composite arrangement.

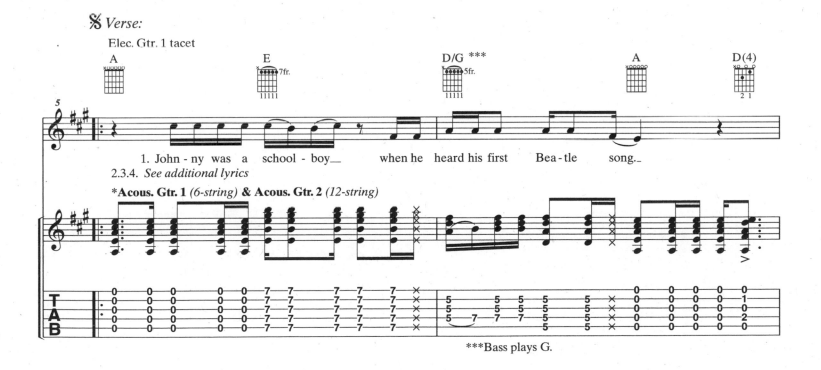

***Bass plays G.

Shooting Star - 11 - 1

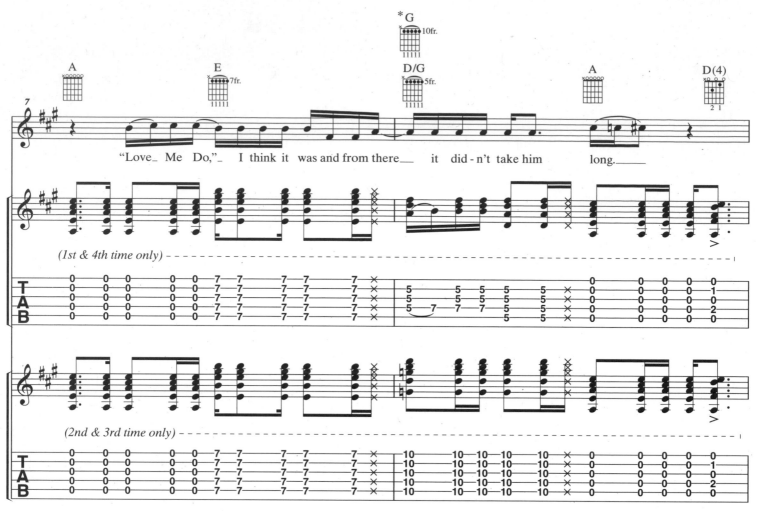

"Love_ Me Do,"_ I think it was and from there___ it did-n't take him long.____

(1st & 4th time only) - |

(2nd & 3rd time only) - |

*Acous. Gtrs. 1 & 2 play G, 2nd and 3rd time only.

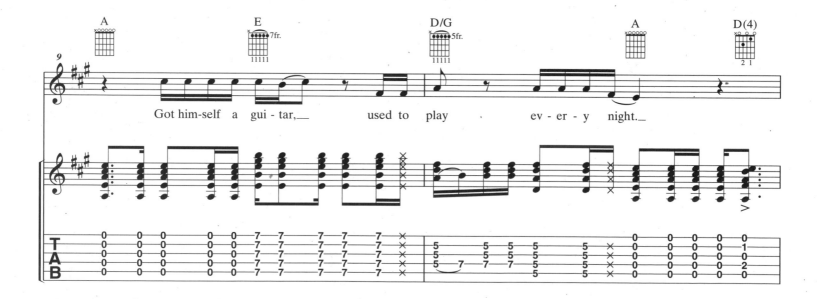

Got him-self a gui-tar,__ used to play ev-er-y night._

*Acous. Gtrs. 1 & 2 play G, 2nd and 3rd time only.
**Elec. Gtrs. 2 & 3 in standard tuning.

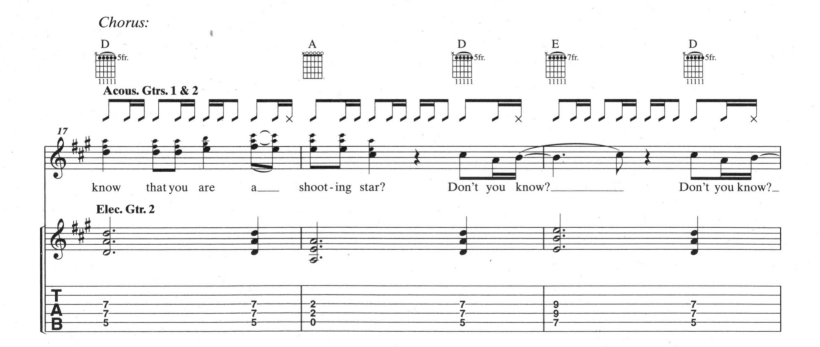

Guitar Solo:

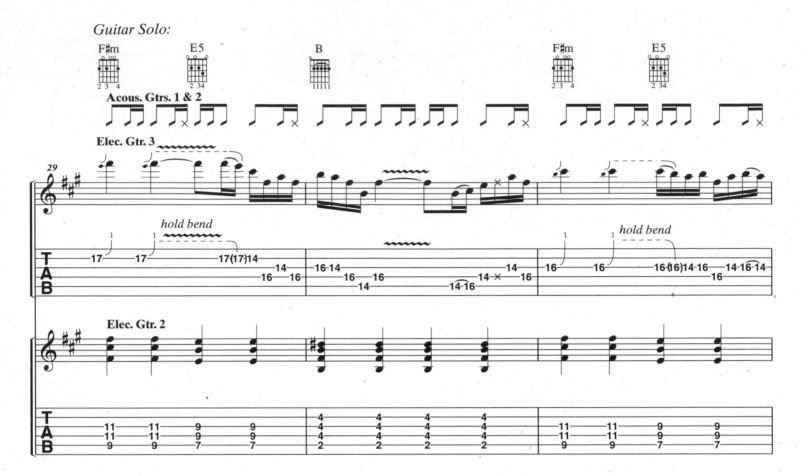

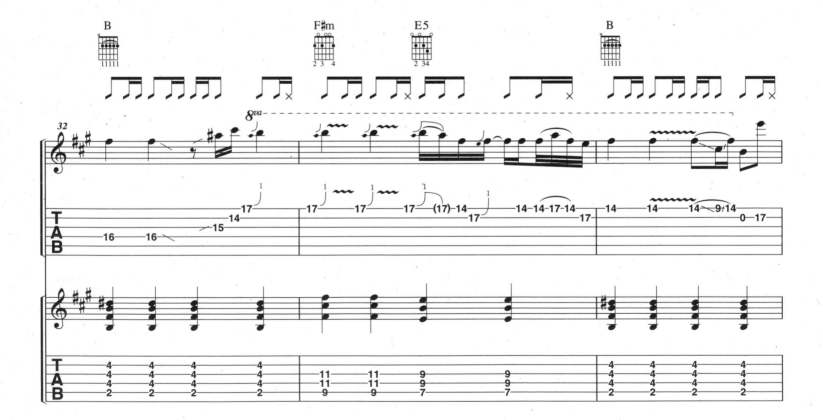

Chorus:

Outro Chorus:
w/Rhy. Fig. 1 *(Acous. Gtrs. 1 & 2) cont. simile to fade*

know_____ that you are_____ a_____ shoot-ing star?

Cont. w/ad lib. vocal

Na, na,

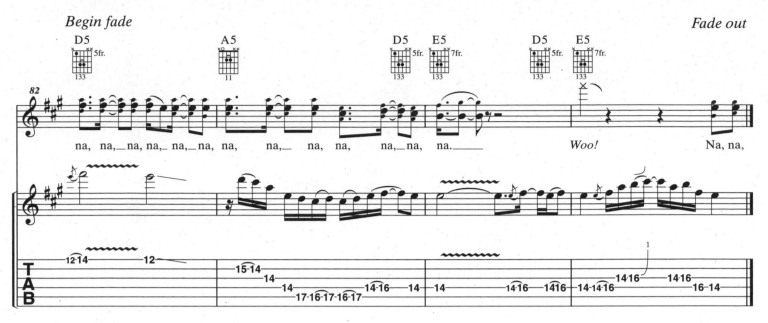

na, na,__na, na,__na,__na, na, na,__ na, na, na,__na, na._____ Woo! Na, na,

Verse 2:
Johnny told his mama,
"Hey, Mama, I'm going away."
I'm gonna hit the big time,
Gonna be a big star someday." Yeah.
Mama came to the door
With a teardrop in her eye.
Johnny said, "Don't cry, Mama,
Smile and wave goodbye."
Don't you know?
Yeah, yeah.
(To Chorus:)

Verse 3:
Johnny made a record,
Went straight up to number one.
Suddenly everyone
Loved to hear him sing his song.
Watching the world go by,
Surprising it goes so fast.
Johnny looked around him and said,
"Well, I made the big time at last."
Don't you know?
Don't you know?
(To Chorus:)

Verse 4:
Johnny died one night,
Died in his bed.
Bottle of whiskey,
Sleeping tablets by his head.
Johnny's life passed him by
Like a warm summer day.
If you listen to the wind you can
Still hear him play.
Oh, whoa, oh.
(To Chorus:)

SIGNS

Words and Music by
LES EMMERSON

Verse:

be here._____ The

Band tacet -------------------------------

*Am G D G

sign said, "You've got to have a mem-ber-ship card to get in-side."__ Uh!

*Chords are implied.

Guitar Solo:

D C G D G D A

Elec. Gtr. 2 resume chorus fig. simile
Elec. Gtr. 1

C D *D.S. % al Coda*

Elec. Gtrs. 1 & 2 3. And the

⊕ *Coda* *Repeat ad lib. and fade*

D C G D G D A C

Elec. Gtr. 1 w/ad lib. fills (use Guitar Solo, meas. 42–45, as a model for improv.)
Elec. Gtr. 2 cont. chorus fig. simile

Sign, sign, ev-'ry-where a sign. Whoo! Sign.

Verse 2:
And the sign said, "Anybody caught trespassin'
Would be shot on sight."
So I jumped on the fence and I yelled at the house,
"Hey! What gives you the right
To put up a fence to keep me out,
But to keep Mother Nature in?
If God was here, he'd tell you to your face,
Man, you're some kind of sinner."
(To Chorus:)

Verse 3:
And the sign said, "Everybody, welcome,
Come in, kneel down and pray."
But when they passed around the plate at the end of it all,
I didn't have a penny to pay.
So I got me a pen and a paper
And I made up my own little sign.
I said, "Thank you, Lord, for thinkin' 'bout me.
I'm alive and doin' fine."
(To Chorus:)

Signs - 4 - 4

SO YOU WANT TO BE
A ROCK AND ROLL STAR

Moderately fast ♩ = 146

Words and Music by
ROGER McGUINN and CHRIS HILLMAN

1. So you want to be a rock 'n' roll star?__ Then lis-ten now__ to what I say.__
2.3. *See additional lyrics*

So You Want to Be a Rock and Roll Star - 2 - 1

Verse 2:
Then it's time to go downtown
Where the agent man won't let you down.
Sell your soul to the company
Who are waiting there to sell plastic ware.

And in a week or two,
If you make the charts,
The girls'll tear you apart.
(To Instrumental:)

Verse 3:
The price you paid for your riches and fame,
Was it all a strange game,
You're a little insane.
The money that came and the public acclaim,
Don't forget what you are,
You're a rock 'n' roll star!

La, la, la…
(To Outro:)

STAIRWAY TO HEAVEN

Words and Music by
JIMMY PAGE and ROBERT PLANT

Stairway to Heaven - 9 - 1

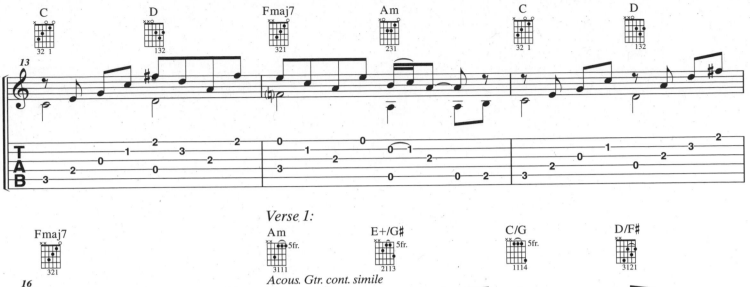

Verse 1:

Stairway to Heaven - 9 - 2

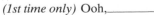

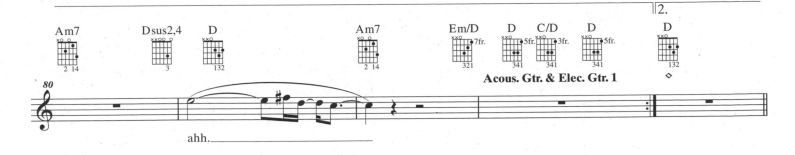

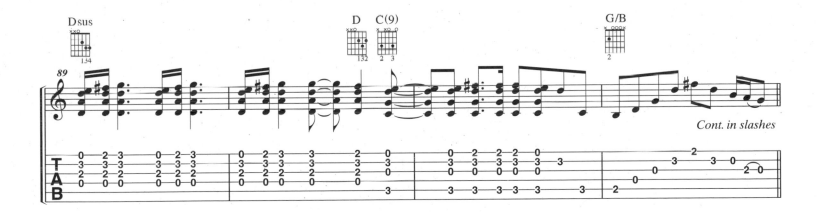

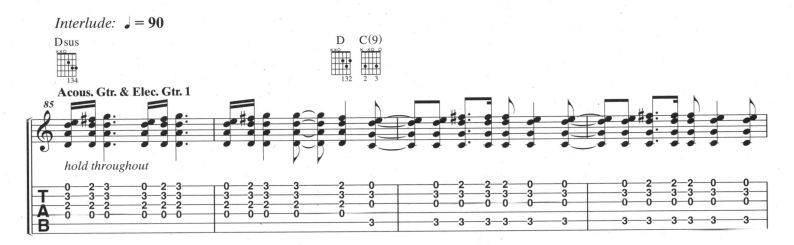

Stairway to Heaven - 9 - 6

248

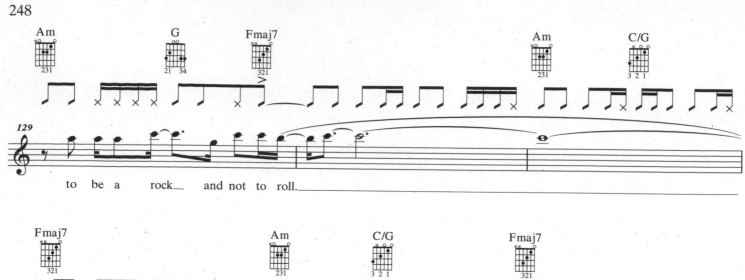

to be a rock__ and not to roll.__

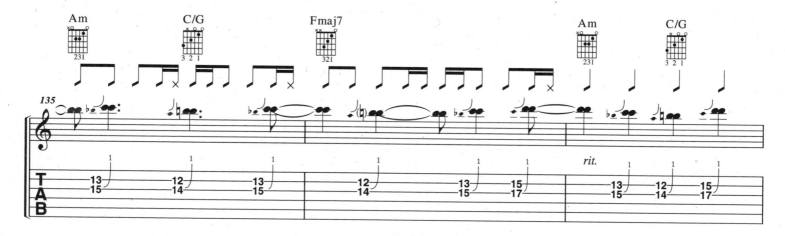

And she's   buy - ing   a   stair - way__   to   heav - en.__

Stairway to Heaven - 9 - 9

STAYIN' ALIVE

Words and Music by
BARRY GIBB, MAURICE GIBB
and ROBIN GIBB

Stayin' Alive - 3 - 1

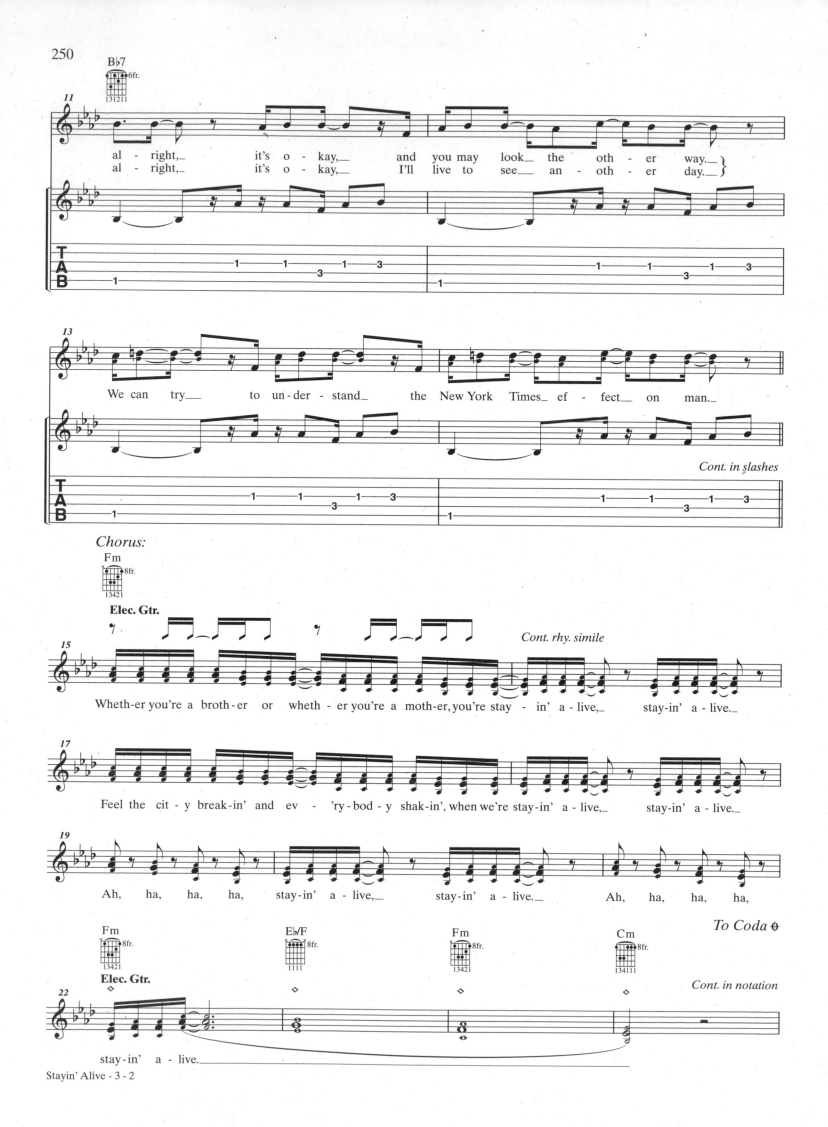

SUNSHINE OF YOUR LOVE

Words and Music by
JACK BRUCE, PETE BROWN
and ERIC CLAPTON

Sunshine of Your Love - 5 - 1

Sunshine of Your Love - 5 - 2

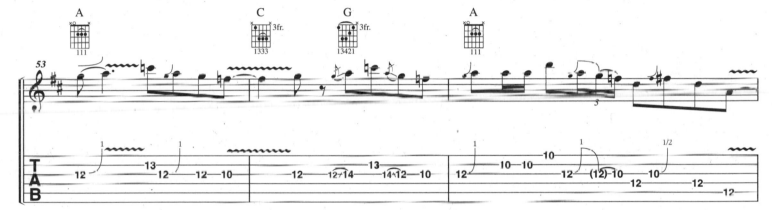

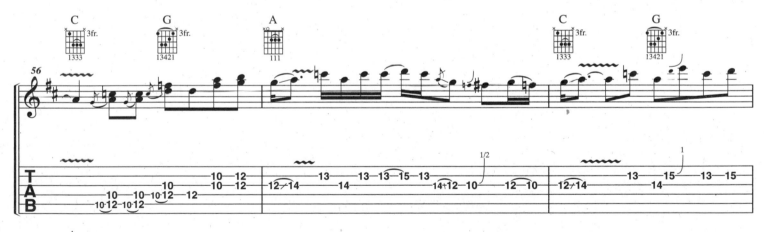

Sunshine of Your Love - 5 - 4

TIN MAN

Words and Music by
DEWEY BUNNELL

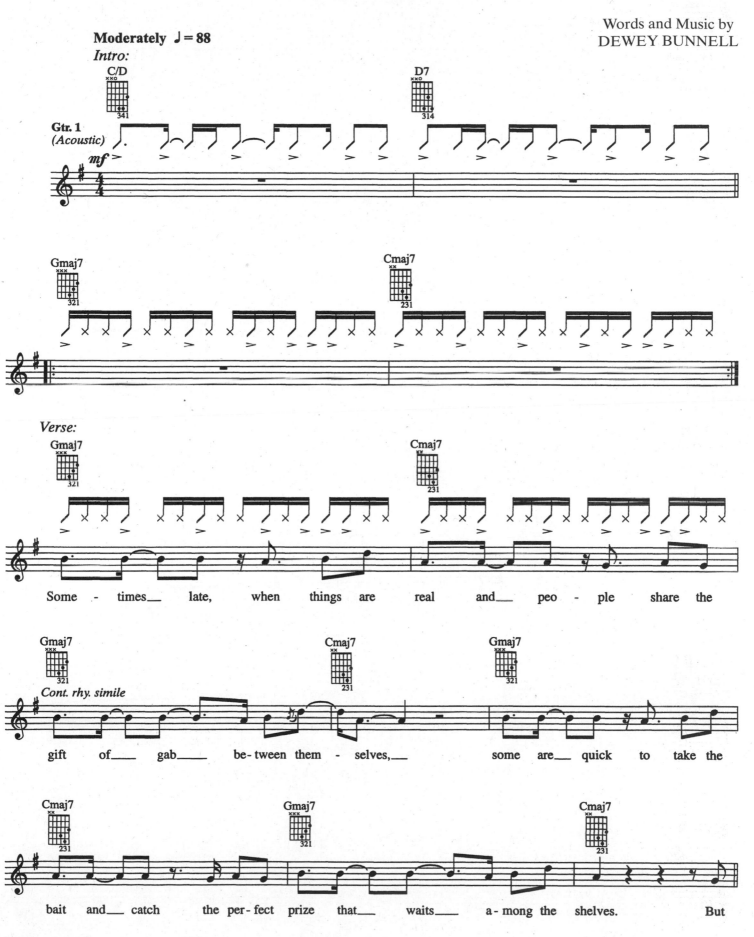

Tin Man - 3 - 1

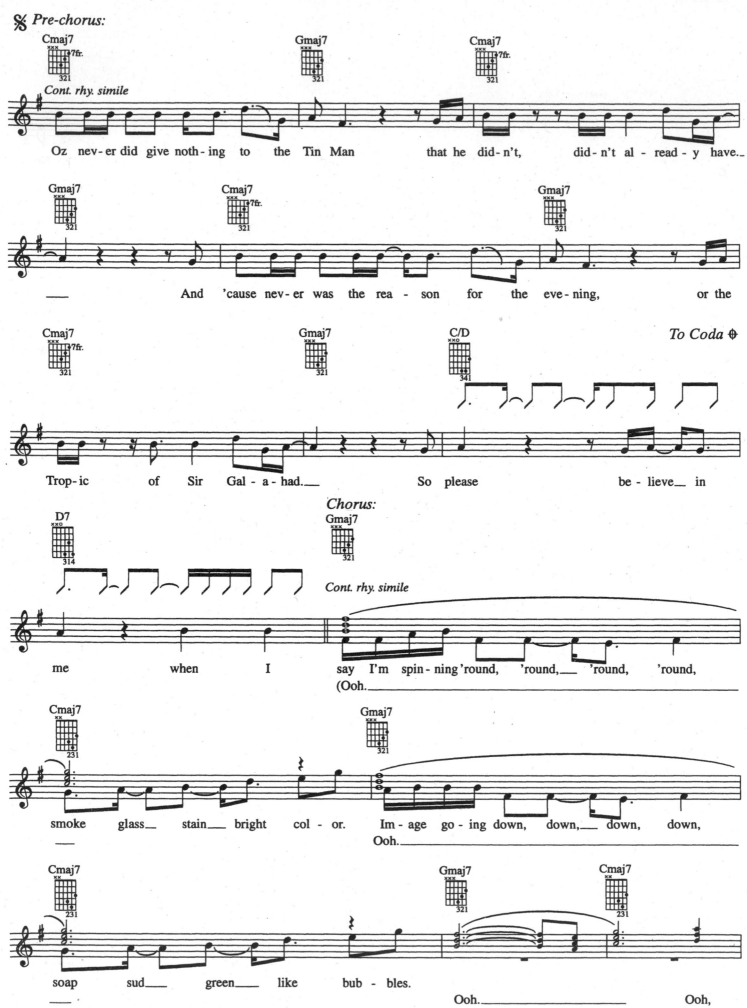

THAT'S ALL RIGHT

Words and Music by
ARTHUR CRUDUP

Lyrics:
1. Well, that's all right, ma-ma, that's all right for you. That's all right, ma-ma, just an-y-way you do. Well, that's all

2.3. See additional lyrics

That's All Right - 4 - 1

right, that's all right. That's all_____

_____ right____ now, ma - ma,_____ an - y - way you do.____

To Coda ⊕ | 1. | 2.

2. Well,

Guitar Solo:

Acous. Gtr. cont. rhy. simile

262

That's All Right - 4 - 3

De, de, de,___ de. De, de, de,___ de, I need your lov-

-in', that's all right. That's all___

right___ now, ma - ma,___ an - y - way you do.___

Acous. Gtr.

Verse 2:
Well, mama she done told me,
Papa done told me too,
"Son, that gal your foolin' with,
She ain't no good for you."
But, that's all right, that's all right.
That's all right now, mama, anyway you do.
(To Guitar Solo:)

Verse 3:
I'm leaving town, baby,
I'm leaving town for sure.
Well, then you won't be bothered with
Me hangin' 'round your door.
But, that's all right, that's all right.
That's all right now, mama, anyway you do.
(To Coda)

GUITAR TAB GLOSSARY

TABLATURE EXPLANATION

TAB illustrates the six strings of the guitar.
Notes and chords are indicated by the placement of fret numbers on each string.

String ⑥, 3rd fret   String ①, 12th fret   A "C" chord   C chord arpeggiated
                     String ③, 13th fret

BENDING NOTES

Half Step:
Play the note and bend string one half step (one fret).

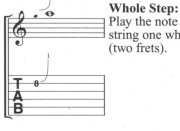

Whole Step:
Play the note and bend string one whole step (two frets).

Slight Bend/ Quarter-Tone Bend:
Play the note and bend string sharp.

Prebend and Release:
Play the already-bent string, then immediately drop it down to the fretted note.

Bend and Release:
Play the note and bend to the next pitch, then release to the original note. Only the first note is attacked.

PICK DIRECTION

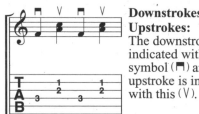

Downstrokes and Upstrokes:
The downstroke is indicated with this symbol (⊓) and the upstroke is indicated with this (V).

ARTICULATIONS

Hammer On:
Play the lower note, then "hammer" your finger to the higher note. Only the first note is plucked.

Pull Off:
Play the higher note with your first finger already in position on the lower note. Pull your finger off the first note with a strong downward motion that plucks the string—sounding the lower note.

Palm Mute:
The notes are muted (muffled) by placing the palm of the pick hand lightly on the strings, just in front of the bridge.

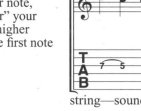

Muted Strings:
A percussive sound is produced by striking the strings while laying the fret hand across them.

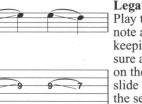

Legato Slide:
Play the first note and, keeping pressure applied on the string, slide up to the second note. The diagonal line shows that it is a slide and not a hammer-on or a pull-off.

HARMONICS

Natural Harmonic:
A finger of the fret hand lightly touches the string at the note indicated in the TAB and is plucked by the pick producing a bell-like sound called a harmonic.

RHYTHM SLASHES

Strum Marks/ Rhythm Slashes:
Strum with the indicated rhythm pattern. Strum marks can be located above the staff or within the staff.

Single Notes with Rhythm Slashes:
Sometimes single notes are incorporated into a strum pattern. The circled number below is the string and the fret number is above.

Artificial Harmonic:
Fret the note at the first TAB number, lightly touch the string at the fret indicated in parens (usually 12 frets higher than the fretted note), then pluck the string with an available finger or your pick.